I
PROMISE
MYSELF

I
PROMISE
MYSELF

Making a Commitment
to Yourself *and* Your Dreams

PATRICIA LYNN REILLY

Foreword by SABRINA WARD HARRISON

CONARI PRESS
Berkeley, California

Conari Press books are distributed by Publishers Group West.

ISBN: 1-57324-178-4

Cover and Book Design: Suzanne Albertson
Cover Photography: Calla Lily, S. Nakamura. Courtesy of Photonica
Author Photo: Helena Leifer

LIBRARY OF CONGRESS CATALOGING-IN-PUBLICATION DATA

Reilly, Patricia Lynn.
    I promise myself : making a commitment to yourself and your dreams /
Patricia Lynn Reilly ; foreword by Sabrina Ward Harrison.
        p.   cm.
    ISBN 1-57324-178-4 (paperback)
        1. Women—Psychology. 2. Self-esteem in women. I. Title.

HQ1206.R43 2000
158.1'082—dc21   00-021264

Printed in the United States of America on recycled paper.

00 01 02 03   DATA REPRO   10 9 8 7 6 5 4 3 2 1

I Promise Myself

FOREWORD

by SABRINA WARD HARRISON, author of *Spilling Open*

hat a blessing Patricia Lynn Reilly is, and her new book, *I Promise Myself: Making a Conscious Commitment to Yourself and Your Dreams*. I had never written a foreword before, and was feeling the "I don't know how to do it right" feeling. The funny thing is, every time I picked up Patricia's book to take notes for the foreword, her words spoke so kindly and encouragingly to me that I would take a big breath and remember again that this book has *found me*. And there is a reason it finds me again and again.

You know those books that are gifts the way a new woman friend is a gift? When you know right away that they "get it"? I treasure the bare honesty. In the presence of these books and these women we know that we can truly be *all* of ourselves. I believe that by these connections we deepen our own knowledge of our stories, our strengths.

Patricia captures me right away by telling her story of being "caught in the swirls of relationships." She begins, "Why do precious women *of any age* surrender so completely to another that they lose themselves? Why did I? . . . Why would I allow another to swallow me up so completely that it's taken six months to recapture myself? . . . God, please don't let this happen to me again. I need time to grasp firmly who I am, my dreams, my life, my future so I will never give myself away again." From this place Patricia leads us through deep commitments, ceremonies, healing writing, a wider sky where our own true and strong selves can dance and rest.

This book found me when I needed it most.

I was lost from myself. Life was more confusing than ever, because so many people around me were saying that they were finding new strength in themselves from reading my first book, *Spilling Open: The Art of Becoming Yourself*. But where had the deep down me gone? The plain and simple, dancing-alone-in-my-room-to-Indigo-Girls Sabrina? The "girl-child" that Patricia describes? I felt like I had given myself away 18,000 times in just a few months—ulcers had filled my stomach like tumbleweeds. God was calling me to stop and feel, listen, care again for *me* . . . me under the surface, where I could speak closely to myself and write notes in my journal to God.

I did listen. I bought a cheap ticket to Italy, to travel alone for a month with a backpack, a tiny set of watercolors, and an empty journal.

I was scared and ready. There was much to experience. I needed to challenge the edges of myself. This trip to Italy at age twenty-three was the greatest gift I have ever given myself. I trusted myself again. *My* decisions were clearer; my solitude was rich and present. Most of the time I wore a kid's Superman T-shirt I bought on the street in Florence, and felt that great "super strong Sab" feeling I had missed since I was a little girl. It wasn't a feeling of material success; it was more of a quiet bold strength. I knew myself again, and with that I could do anything.

This book wants to be shared. It calls to quiet bed reading and also to circles of women reading and laughing out loud, with a big *Yes!* of agreement. This sharing brings understanding of what we all struggle with, and we can help one another heal and grow deeper into our authentic strength. *I Promise Myself* has inspired me to form a woman's group to follow along with it so we can share the book and our stories together.

Welcome inside. May you be touched by your truth as much as I was.

An Invitation to Be True to Yourself

Imagine a woman who has grown in knowledge and love of herself. A woman who has vowed faithfulness to her life and capacities. Who remains loyal to herself. Regardless. Imagine yourself as this woman.

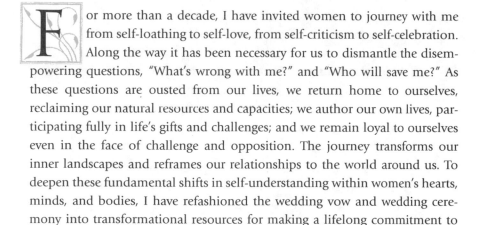

For more than a decade, I have invited women to journey with me from self-loathing to self-love, from self-criticism to self-celebration. Along the way it has been necessary for us to dismantle the disempowering questions, "What's wrong with me?" and "Who will save me?" As these questions are ousted from our lives, we return home to ourselves, reclaiming our natural resources and capacities; we author our own lives, participating fully in life's gifts and challenges; and we remain loyal to ourselves even in the face of challenge and opposition. The journey transforms our inner landscapes and reframes our relationships to the world around us. To deepen these fundamental shifts in self-understanding within women's hearts, minds, and bodies, I have refashioned the wedding vow and wedding ceremony into transformational resources for making a lifelong commitment to ourselves. Each woman's journey culminates in the composition of a "vow of faithfulness" to herself, which is then witnessed at a commitment ceremony.

Although I have developed many effective resources and tools of support over the years, none has been as universally understood and as powerfully experienced as the vow-composition process. Once a woman recognizes that a healthy and vibrant relationship with herself is the prerequisite to healthy and vibrant relationships with others, she transfers her knowledge about wedding vows—whether her own or someone else's—to the process of composing a vow to herself. Just as most couples consider it essential to express their love and devotion in a formal vow witnessed at a public ceremony, so too are women expressing their self-love and self-commitment in "vows of faithfulness" and inviting friends and chosen family to witness them. The results are life altering:

- ∾ High-school-aged women are vowing faithfulness to their own lives. As a result, they are focusing their astounding life energy on the exploration of their interests and curiosities and the development of their gifts and talents. Kathy wrote her vow during her senior year in high school. It became her guiding light during the disorienting and sometimes overwhelming first year of college. Her vow inspired her to participate fully in the challenges of college life, using them as an opportunity to sharpen her skills for conscious living and to deepen her partnership with herself.

- ∾ Twentysomething women are vowing faithfulness to their own lives. As a result, their relationship obsession is dissolving. The organizing focus of twenty-year-old Susan's life is no longer the pursuit of lovers; it is maintaining her vow of faithfulness to herself. Susan refuses to measure her success or failure as a woman by her ability to "snag" a husband; she now defines success as the fulfillment of her own potential.

∞ Engaged women are vowing faithfulness to their own lives. As a result, they are truly prepared to enter marriage. Sandy, twenty-eight, felt stuck. While trying to write her vows to Nathan, no words would come. Instead, she wrote a vow of faithfulness to herself. Once completed, her vow to Nathan flowed without effort. When faced with a challenge in her marriage, Sandy reviews and then renews her personal vow.

∞ Women in transition because of divorce or the death of a partner are vowing faithfulness to their own lives. As a result, they are remembering their personal dreams and goals. Sixty-year-old Helen was married at eighteen. She spent the next forty years supporting her husband's career until he died unexpectedly. While writing her vow of faithfulness, Helen remembered her own dream of becoming a pediatric nurse and vowed to fulfill it.

Women of all ages, from all walks of life, are vowing faithfulness to their own lives. As a result, they are refusing to ask the questions "What's wrong with me?" and "Who will save me?" Instead, they make powerful statements with every thought they share, every feeling they express, and every action they take on their own behalf. They use their personal and communal resources to give birth to woman-affirming rites of passage and ceremonies of transformation for their daughters, granddaughters, nieces, and for themselves. They are women—full of themselves!

This book provides step-by-step guidelines for composing your personal vow of faithfulness. The vow-composition process invites you to turn inward and reestablish a committed relationship to yourself. By accepting the invitation, you will be offering yourself what was needed most during childhood and adolescence: support to go on a remarkable adventure of self-discovery, deepening your relationship to your vitality, resilience, and sense of self. Throughout the book I have included the stories of women and their vows. May their words inspire you to grow in knowledge and love of yourself, to vow faithfulness to your natural resources and capacities, and to remain loyal to yourself. Regardless.

ONE

Something Old, Something New: Refashioning the Wedding Vow and Ceremony

Caught in the swirling actions, thoughts, and journeys of others, we lose touch with our breath, our bodies, and the grounding center within us. All who have lost their way, come. Serenity awaits you here. Rediscover the way home.

Several high school and college-aged young women told their stories on *Oprah!* the other day. Caught in the life-threatening swirls of possessive, jealous, and controlling boyfriends, these women represent, according to statistics, one out of every four young American women. Whirling in a chaos not their own, unable to get their bearings, some had lost years of their lives—important, irreplaceable years. While their classmates were testing the limits of their intellectual capacities and exploring their interests and curiosities in order to discern a direction, a calling, a career, a focus for their astounding life energy and potential, these young women lost all interest in themselves, their friends, their studies, and their futures. They told us about the contraction of their lives to meet the demands, fulfill the expectations, and obey the dictates of their jealous lovers:

"He tells me whom I can see and whom I can't see."

By the time they are seventeen many young women have surrendered their ambitions to a growing need for affection and their autonomy to an emotional dependence on the approval and good will of others. At seventeen the young woman is well on her way to being a formula female.
—MADONNA KOLBENSCHLAG,
KISS SLEEPING BEAUTY GOOD-BYE

"I have to check in with him on the hour or he gets angry."

"He broke my pager so no one else can contact me."

"He wants me to dress a certain way based on his preferences. I have no choice in the matter."

"If another boy talks to me, he holds me responsible. He is very jealous. I can't have male friends."

I was horrified as they told their stories. How can this happen in 1999, when Madeleine Albright is negotiating humanitarian interventions and peace agreements around the world, when the players of the Women's National Basketball Association are inspiring a generation of Title IX young women, and when Oprah herself is offering women and girls transformational resources daily on national TV? How can this be in so-called postfeminist America, where we're told all the battles have been won and true gender equality is at hand? Oprah asked the resident "expert" my question. The expert reminded the audience that one out of four adult women is in an abusive relationship—like mother, like daughter. More profoundly, young women in our culture are convinced by the age of twelve that the pursuit and maintenance of a relationship with a man should be their number one life priority, a priority that can easily turn into an obsession with life-threatening consequences. How can this be? And yet there it was, poignantly portrayed on national TV—out of four young women were facing the same old challenges in 1999 as there counterparts had in 1969, 1959, 1949.

I posed my question to three young women in high school: "Hasn't anything *really* changed for you? Were all our efforts to make your way less turbulent, more self-respecting, in vain?" They reminded me of the magazines they read, the ads they see, and the music they hear daily—words and images proclaiming with greater tenacity and effectiveness than the images of women in the State Department, on basketball courts, and yes, more loudly even than the woman-affirming programming of Harpo Productions, that *girls need to be saved* and that *boys are the saviors*. Hannah spoke for all of them: "If we became as powerful as

It's important for girls to explore the impact the culture has on their growth and development. They all benefit from, to use an old-fashioned term, consciousness raising. Once girls understand the effects of the culture on their lives, they can fight back. They learn that they have conscious choices to make and ultimate responsibility for those choices. Intelligent resistance keeps the true self alive.
—MARY PIPHER, REVIVING OPHELIA

Madeleine Albright or as smart as Oprah Winfrey, what man would ever want us? Boys like girls who don't have it all together, girls who know they need to be saved."

I asked Hannah, Juliet, and Jennifer if the words of a woman who attended high school forty years ago in 1959 described their experience today: "I expected men to save me from loneliness, social disapproval, boredom, failure, and mechanical breakdowns. I have treated men as godlike. This never seemed wrong to me since I've been surrounded by women who go to extremes to please their men at all stages of life." Yes, they told me, young women today expect their boyfriends to save them from the same things. They added "being homeless" and "harassment from other boys" to the list and then laughed nervously. Jennifer explained, "Sometimes the savior becomes the harasser. All of us have friends whose lives have been threatened by their boyfriends." I asked why girls don't leave when the relationship becomes abusive. Juliet answered, "Respectability comes from having a boyfriend whether he's nice or mean. To leave is shameful and sometimes dangerous. And it's not all that different for our moms. I asked my mom to leave her second husband over and over again. It's obvious he's using her and I don't feel comfortable around him. She really doesn't believe she can survive without a man. I've stopped asking."

Any transitional time in a girl's life is a delicate opportunity for growth, a time of heightened vulnerability which signals the emergence of a potential strength. Ritual affirmation at these critical junctures helps her cross the next developmental threshold.
—VIRGINIA BEANE RUTTER, *CELEBRATING GIRLS*

One young women didn't make it to *Oprah!* that day to tell her story. Instead her father told viewers about the night she was picked up by her boyfriend. They drove to his apartment for a "breaking up" ritual, returning each other's CDs and other valuable items exchanged during their relationship. This sweet young woman believed they could remain

4

friends, right up until her final breath. With "If I can't have you, no one else will," her life was taken by a possessive lover. Her precious spirit lives on in her father's ministry among young women and men. He tells his daughter's story. He hopes some lives are saved in memory of her.

Imagine our young women growing in knowledge and love of themselves. Young women vowing faithfulness to their own lives and capacities. Young women remaining loyal to themselves—regardless. Imagine an adolescence in which our daughters, granddaughters, and nieces deepen their relationship to their natural vitality, resilience, and sense of self. Imagine a girl-affirming rite of passage, a ceremony of commitment to themselves, culminating with these words of self-blessing: "This is it. This is my life. Nothing to wait for. Nowhere else to go. No one to make it all different. What a relief to have finally landed here . . . now. Blessed be my life!"

Caught in the Swirls

Why do precious women *of any age* surrender so completely to another that they lose themselves? Why did I? My story is typical. In my twenties, I became aware of a pattern in my relationships with food and men, and with my own inner world of memories, thoughts, and feelings. I noticed that these relationships had a swirling quality about them. It was as if I had no solid ground to stand upon. I was forever swirling

A single affirmative act between a woman and a girl, on behalf of the feminine, ripples out to larger and larger groups of girls and women in our culture.
—VIRGINIA BEANE RUTTER,
CELEBRATING GIRLS

in someone else's life or caught in the tangled web of my own swirling inner life.

My first swirling relationship was with my alcoholic parents. I had no choice but to get caught up in navigating within the swirl of their addictions. It became an all-consuming task. Little life energy was left over for my own healthy development. In addition, I, as a girl-child, was encouraged to get caught up in the actions, thoughts, feelings, and journeys of others. As a result, I assumed inappropriate responsibility for the cause, modification, and outcome of the choices, behaviors, and actions of others, and I carried this ineffective behavior into each relationship.

As a young adult, I married and continued the patterns of childhood by becoming caught up in the swirls of a newly sober alcoholic. I felt responsible for his sobriety: If only I was a good and loving enough wife, he would not drink. Focusing on his actions, thoughts, and feelings distracted me from attending to my own challenges, concerns, and recovery. Needless to say, my overinvolvement in his life became intolerable to my husband. And because I had lost track of myself, I was no longer available for true intimacy. The marriage ended.

After the divorce, I avoided alcoholics, but became involved in the swirls of a series of men whose temperament was similar to my father's. Dan was the first. We met at the card catalog in the graduate school library. From the moment we met, I knew my heart had attached to him in a way that was both exhilarating and frightening. I wrote in my journal that evening: "My heart, persistent in its ways, has been drawn again to a man with Daddy's energy—a familiar energy. Will this

Instead of planting our solitude with our own dream blossoms, we choke the space with continuous music, chatter, and companionship. When the noise stops, there is no inner music to take its place. We must relearn to be alone.
—ANNE MORROW LINDBERGH,
GIFTS FROM THE SEA

6

man of passion leave as Daddy did? Will I ever experience passion's permanence with such a one?"

Although aware of the pattern and its potential danger, I persisted: Dan, the lost one who must be found; Dan, whose brilliance must be uncovered and fanned to life. Soon we were eating every meal together and studying together at the library, usually at my initiative. My life became completely absorbed into his dreams, his pain, his journey. One day Dan left, just as my father had done many years before. Six months after his dramatic departure, I wrote these words in my journal: "I must understand why I gave up a year of my life to him. Why would I allow another to swallow me up so completely that it's taken six months to recapture myself? I am frightened to see him because he symbolizes my lost year caught in the swirl of his pain, choices, and dreams. God, please don't let this happen to me again. I need time to firmly grasp who I am, my dreams, my life, my future, so I will never give myself away again. I'm petrified of becoming lost in someone else's life; yet, I'm just as afraid of holding onto my life. Having no home of my own and petrified of diving into the uncharted territory of my own inner life, am I destined to wander from one swirling man to another? Will I ever find rest within myself?"

In the pauses between relationships, I ate compulsively. I literally hid in closets to eat and dropped out of life for months at a time. Without someone's swirl to engage in, I was at a loss. In the pauses, I was reminded of my swirling inner life of unexpressed feelings, unacknowledged memories, and untapped potential. I ate to quiet the feelings and to eradicate any reminders of the past. To live the life of another made perfect sense. The prospect of living my own life frightened me. I ate to avoid the awesome responsibility of coming home to myself.

Pause for a moment and consider this definition: "A swirl is any relationship or person; religion, cause, or dogma; food or drug; or activity or project outside of oneself that becomes the controlling or organizing focus of one's time, energy, and attention." What was the controlling or organizing focus of your time, energy, and attention in childhood? Your parents' moods or addictions? The care of your siblings? Receiving adults' approval and validation? What is the controlling or organizing focus of your time, energy, and attention today? Your partner's moods? The dramas of your siblings? The addictions of your adult children? Your boyfriend's demands? The "body-beautiful" expectations of the culture? The quest for a savior?

In the Fullness of Time

During a chaplaincy training seminar, we were told this story: A camper noticed a moth pushing, straining, and struggling to get out of its cocoon. It was a disturbing sight to the camper, and when she could take it no longer, she extended the tiny slit-opening of the cocoon. The moth was freed. It fell to the ground and died. The camper was devastated. Her intention had been to help.

Inspired by the story, I investigated the moth's life. Its life cycle from egg to adult moth is orchestrated by a remarkable inner mechanism of "right timing" that leads to each new transformation. This inner timing allows for the emergence of the larva to coincide with an adequate food supply, for the outgrowing of each of its skins, and for the location and creation of the cocoon, where it will remain in a state of lethargy until the conditions are ready for its survival as a fully formed adult moth. The struggle against the walls of the cocoon supports the moth's metamorphosis by strengthening its wings and releasing fluids to enhance its coloring. The camper, unaware of the importance of timing and the sacredness of struggle in the moth's cycle, cut open the cocoon. This premature release led to the moth's death. Swirling in her own discomfort, the camper had arrogantly intruded in the moth's life process. Yet the moth was content in the midst of its own trustworthy process, a process essential to its development.

Like the moth, each of us is an emerging healthy adult whose process is orchestrated by a finely tuned inner timing. In the fullness of time, when a behavior begins to hamper, press, and squeeze us, we twist and turn until we burst out of the old skin and are freed into a deeper level of our existence. Each time a memory or feeling is ready to be acknowledged after decades of denial, it gnaws its way to the surface through a dream or a sensory memory, through a movie, or by reading the stories of others. In the fullness of time, it is remembered or felt. The trustworthy timing of our Inner Wisdom leads us to each new transformation when we are ready.

In my desperate attempts to manage the swirls of others and to quiet my own swirling inner world of childhood memories and emotions, my energy was depleted. And yet my swirling didn't stop until it was ready. Swirls have a life and purpose of their own. They are held within a trustworthy process. *In the fullness of time,* I became dizzy. This dizziness was essential. Unable to eat or sleep, fragile and shaking, I became willing to journey home to myself and to take full responsibility for my own life and its rich potential.

In the fullness of time, I entered Al-Anon, overwhelmed by the swirls of my newly sober husband's recovery. Years later, swirling in the "familiar energy" of daddy-shaped lovers, clutching the few remaining pieces of my life, I reached out to a circle of women. *In the fullness of time,* exhausted by the swirls of compulsive overeating and bingeing, I enrolled in yet another support group. *In the fullness of time,* caught in the swirl of my family history intruding in my present life, I contacted a counselor. I was tired of my unacknowledged past silently affecting the present. I was ready to listen to my childhood memories and to heal into the present.

Dizzy, I stumbled into the counselor's office, the circle of women, and countless self-help meetings. I was offered information, insight, and tools of support. I was inspired by the experience, strength, and hope of women who were detaching from the swirls of others and turning toward their own lives. I became willing to journey home to the feelings, memories, and inner life that had been clamoring for my attention. I was being drawn inward to reestablish a relationship to myself, yet I had forgotten the way home.

> *Pause for a moment and acknowledge the "dizziness" that prompted you to seek out a support group, a women's circle, or a therapist. How did you experience the dizziness in your body, breath, and inner life? Did you ignore your body's health and well-being? Was your breath shallow, seldom reaching into your abdomen? Were your personal projects set aside due to frantic-ness and exhaustion? Have you become willing to journey home to yourself and take full responsibility for your own life and its rich potential?*

The Descent

A skillful therapist was my first escort into the rich resources of my inner life. In her office I descended into my "swirling" inner life and discovered unused capacities, unexpressed needs, and unexplored sexual potential; discarded thoughts, disregarded feelings, untapped creative impulses, and unexpressed longings for both solitude and acknowledgment. My inner life was in disarray due to years of inattention and, initially, the accumulation of a lifetime frightened me. During our two years together, however, I learned to trust my inner life, to discern its intricate design, and to listen to its healing truth. I discovered that the deepest impulse of my being was to heal into the present. As I descended into my own life, I reconnected to this impulse and tapped a reservoir of transformative resources.

As I befriended the richness within me and reclaimed my own natural resources, I redirected my energy away from the "swirling" patterns of old and toward adventures of self-discovery. Recognizing each impulse to step into the life of another as an indication of disconnection from myself, I learned to pause, notice the disconnection without judgment, and then return home, making conscious contact with my breath, woman-body, and inner life—faithful escorts on my journey home to myself. In this way I reestablished the connection with myself. No longer denying any aspect of myself, I tapped into my own self-healing capacities as deeper layers of inner truth and wisdom became available to me. I was growing in knowledge and love of myself.

Although the process of self-discovery was compelling, I became aware of a disturbing pattern. I was unable to sustain interest in my own life and creativity for more than three to five months. I would then create a distraction, usually in the form of another "swirling" relationship. While in the relationship, I would lose touch with myself again. I personalized the words of the noted feminist psychologist Jean Baker Miller during this season of life: "I am capable of moving out of a position of inability and of exerting effective action in my own behalf. Yet I become frightened of the implications of this new and empowering vision of myself. I pull back and refuse to follow through on the new course, saying to myself: 'If I can determine the direction of my own life rather than give it over to others, can I exist with satisfaction? And who will ever love me, or even tolerate me, if I do that?'"

Exhausted by this pattern, I wanted a time out from intimate relationships to allow the fragile knowledge and love of myself to root deeply within the ground of my being. I decided to "marry myself," to vow faithfulness to my own life. Supported by a circle of women, I chose to abstain from sexually intimate relationships for two years. In preparation, I wrote my first "vow of faithfulness" based on the resources and capacities discovered as I descended into the richness of my own life:

I, Patricia Lynn Reilly, in response to the truth, in love with myself, full of boldness and grace, express my vow of faithfulness with these words:

I will love my body all the days of my life, touching it with tenderness and supporting it with strength. I will honor its rhythms and cycles as an exquisite resource. I will honor the body of the goddess in my changing body.

I will listen to the deep wisdom of my body all the days of my life. I will meet its needs with tenderness and grace, designing the shape of my days in accordance with its feedback. I will eat

> It has long been recognized that people sometimes have what are called "negative therapeutic reactions." This means that they make a major gain and then seem to get worse after it. Many of these reactions are depressions and they occur when a person has made a major step toward taking on responsibility and direction in her own life. The person has seen that she can move out of a position of inability and can exert effective action in her own behalf, but then becomes frightened of the implications of that new vision. She then pulls back and refuses to follow through on the new course.
> —JEAN BAKER MILLER,
> TOWARD A NEW PSYCHOLOGY FOR WOMEN

foods that support its vitality, drink water to moisten its capacities, and sleep well to renew its life energy.

I will embrace my sexuality as my own all the days of my life. I will delight in pleasuring myself, exploring the edges of my sensuality. I will trust my body's clear "Yes" and "No" in the choice of lovers.

I will honor the whole range of human emotion all the days of my life. I will circulate my feelings, allowing them to pass through me as gracefully as a breath. I will take responsibility for meeting my own emotional needs, enlisting the support of respectful friends and chosen family.

I will speak my truth all the days of my life. I will tell the untold truths of a lifetime to my lovers, colleagues, and friends. I will assume intellectual equality by refusing to defer to the thoughts and perceptions of others.

I will love my creative impulses all the days of my life. I will give expression daily to the words, shapes, images, and movements that emerge from within me. I will celebrate my unique vision and experience, refusing to color inside someone else's lines.

I will sustain interest in myself all the days of my life. I will befriend the solitude of my own life. I will embrace my own life as teacher, healer, and challenge, valuing its lessons above the prescriptions of experts.

Woman must come of age by herself.
—ANNE MORROW LINDBERGH,
GIFTS FROM THE SEA

I will choose to be full of myself all the days of my life. I will honor my desire for acknowledgment and recognition, surrounding myself with friends who applaud my fullness.

Pause for a moment and imagine growing in knowledge and love of yourself, vowing faithfulness to your own life and capacities, and remaining loyal to yourself—regardless. Imagine a life in which you deepen your relationship to your natural vitality, resilience, and sense of self. Imagine a ceremony of commitment to yourself, culminating with these words of self-blessing: "This is it. This is my life. Nothing to wait for. Nowhere else to go. No one to make it all different. What a relief to have finally landed here ... now. Blessed be my life!"

The Gifts of Solitude

Although initially uncomfortable, the two-year abstinence turned out to be the most valuable gift I have ever given myself. By the end of the time, my commitment to myself and my natural resources and capacities had rooted deeply within the ground of my being. I was comfortable with my solitude. I had developed the navigational tools necessary to return "home" again if I wandered away from myself. Yes, distractions would continue to beckon—thus is the nature of life. Yet I was learning the life practice of noticing distraction without judgment and then returning, always returning home to myself. My grandma's ring, which I wear, reminds me of my vow and escorts me home when I wander away from myself.

Grounded in my own life, supported by a circle of women, I concentrated on two areas of professional development during the season of abstinence. Determined to give as many hours of attention, creativity, and support to women as I had given to men, I developed my ministry among women and designed a business capable of holding the full range of my creative adventures: from workshop facilitation, event production, and resource design to writing books and performing sacred dramas. Determined to write as many pages in service of my own professional life as I had written to the men whose swirls inspired hundreds of pages of poems, exhortations, sermons, and manipulations, I outlined eight writing projects, secured an agent, and sold my first book to a publisher. Since then I have written three more books. I imagine them as daughters, born of the vow of faithfulness to myself.

Finally at rest in my own life and creativity, I was eager to explore intimate relationships. From a place of fullness, I was drawn to a different kind of man: one who took responsibility for his own emotional, spiritual, and practical needs; one who had chosen a wide circle of support and maintained it. No longer willing to give men my total attention, I discovered a middle space in which it was possible to honor my own needs, interests, and projects, *and* to be significantly involved with a partner. Incorporating the cumulative wisdom of my life and the precious insights of my journey of self-discovery, I wrote my second vow. Its purpose was to clarify the qualities essential in a partner, to hold me accountable to my new vision, and to provide a checklist with which to evaluate potential partners. This vow continues to escort me home when I wander away from what is deeply wise for me in the choice of partners:

We are all in the last analysis alone. And this basic state of solitude is not something we have any choice about. It is not something that one can take or leave. We are solitary. We may delude ourselves and act as though it were not so. That is all. But how much better it is to realize that we are so, yes, even to begin by assuming it. Naturally, we will turn giddy.
—RAINER MARIA RILKE,
  LETTERS TO A YOUNG POET

My past remains within me. I have acknowledged it. I have walked through it. I am healing into the present. I will choose partners who are aware of the past's influence on the present. Who have faithfully walked through the past. Who are aware of their historic vulnerabilities and challenges, and who take responsibility for them.

I have worked hard to be able to breathe into this moment without the clutter of an unresolved past and without projection into an unknown future. I love the moment and its unfolding. I will choose partners who are aware, attentive, and available in this moment. Who stay in touch with their feelings, needs, and desires. Who acknowledge what is true for them in the moment.

I delight in feeling a full range of emotions. Without tightening, I breathe into each feeling. It offers me precious information about myself and my responses to the experiences of life. I will choose partners who have befriended their feelings and are able to articulate them. Partners who do not categorize feelings as good or bad. All feelings will be welcomed in the relationship.

I am awake to my life. I pay attention to it. It is my teacher, healer, and challenge. I dance, draw, and write through its challenges, lessons, and healing. I will choose partners who do not use drugs of any type. Partners who are awake to life and pay attention to it. Who embrace its gifts, lessons, and challenges.

Do not allow yourself to be imprisoned by any affection. Keep your solitude. To love purely is to consent to distance. It is to adore the distance between ourselves and that which we love.
—SIMONE WEIL, *GRAVITY AND GRACE*

I am playful, energetic, and alert. I have reclaimed my original vitality. I am unwilling to use my precious life energy in managing crisis and conflict. Instead, I choose graceful relationships that deepen in satisfaction and contentment without depleting my creativity and joy. I will choose partners for whom crisis and conflict are not their drugs of choice. Partners who have developed the relationship skills necessary to dance gracefully through challenging moments. Who are committed to a joyful life.

I am accountable to certain principles of living I have gathered through my association with the recovery, psychology, Quaker, Unitarian, and women's communities. I will choose partners who are accountable to a vision that is larger, deeper, and wider than themselves. Partners who consult this vision, whether it is a set of principles, spiritual practices, psychological understandings, or tools for living. Partners who are not lone rangers.

I have reclaimed the wellspring of creativity within me. Daily, it flows through me in song, movement, poetry, essays, letters, workshops, meditations, retreats, and creative relationships. I will choose partners who are in touch with their own creativity. Partners who welcome and encourage shared creative adventures.

No matter how much women prefer to lean, to be protected and supported, nor how much men desire to have them do so, they must make the voyage of life alone, and for safety in an emergency, they must know something of the laws of navigation. To guide our own craft, we must be captain, pilot, engineer; with chart and compass to stand at the wheel; to watch the winds and waves, and know when to take in the sail, and to read the signs in the firmament over all. It matters not whether the solitary voyager is man or woman; nature, having endowed them equally, leaves them to their own skill and judgment in the hour of danger, and, if not equal to the occasion, alike they perish.
—ELIZABETH CADY STANTON,
"THE SOLITUDE OF SELF"

My body has healed. I have reclaimed my original erotic potential. There is nothing to hide. There is nothing to withhold. All will be accepted. I will choose partners who are willing to explore the depth and breadth of sexual intimacy. Partners who say "Yes" to all that rises between us. Who let go into the dance of our affection.

In circles of women, I have healed of the self-criticism that accompanies women's aging. Today I refuse to use my precious life energy disguising the signs of aging. Rather, I celebrate the accumulation of my years and wisdom, and the changes in my body and life. I will choose relationships with women and men who have the courage and depth to embrace all of who I am and will become in the next decades of my life. I will choose partners who celebrate the fullness of my years, experience, power, and wisdom.

Pause to consider this statement: "Our capacity to love others is in direct proportion to how deeply we love ourselves." As a woman gazes with loving kindness upon her past and present, her body and its needs, her ideas and emotions, her resources and capacities, her injury and exquisite potential, her capacity to love others deepens. Are you willing to gaze upon yourself with loving kindness?

TWO

Growing in Knowledge and Love of Yourself:
The Essential Vow of Faithfulness for All Women

Our beloved planet is in desperate need of women who have
moved from self-loathing to self-love, from self-criticism to self-
celebration. Women who have vowed faithfulness to their own
lives and capacities. Women who use their personal and communal
resources to give birth to woman-affirming rites of passage and
ceremonies of transformation for their daughters, granddaughters,
and nieces, and for themselves. Women—in love with themselves!

he wedding ceremony is a sacred drama that captures our imaginations, evokes our emotions, enlivens our senses, and transforms our reality, for an hour . . . or for a lifetime. All of us have attended such a ceremony as part of a couple's community of support, have gathered together in sacred time and space to witness the public expression of their love, and to hold them accountable to their truest intentions. While sitting there, we imagine our daughter's wedding; we remember our own; we relish the pageantry of color, fragrance, and sound; and we hope against all hope that the noble words spoken, expressing humankind's highest aspirations about love and faithfulness, will come true.

All of us have witnessed the hope-filled vows of couples, acknowledging the love that brought them together and expressing their intention to sustain

Rituals speak the language of the soul. During meaningful ritual, divine energy is absorbed not only by our brains but in our hearts and souls as well. Creating and taking part in a ceremony, whether a solitary blessing or a grand pageant, opens our hearts, connects us with our community, and makes us more accessible to ourselves, others, and God.
—SUE PATTON THOELE,
THE WOMAN'S BOOK OF SOUL

that love over time. Many of us have written our own wedding vows and spoken them aloud to our beloved. Our spoken vow, witnessed by friends and family, reminds us to keep our promises one day at a time. Sadly, many of us did not keep the promises we spoke in hopeful and eager tones on our wedding day. Relationships are complex and require a great deal of skillfulness. Yet lessons on how to cultivate healthy intimate relationships were not included in our official education. We learned what we know from observing our parents. Thus we often carry ineffective behaviors into our intimate relationships—behaviors that contribute to the break-up of one out of every two marriages.

Even more fundamental than our lack of "intimacy" training, we as women were not encouraged to cultivate relationships with *ourselves*—the prerequisite for healthy relationships with others. On the contrary, by adolescence, our relationship to self becomes injured, as described by Carol Gilligan in *Meetings at the Crossroads:* "For over a century, the edge of adolescence has been identified as a time of heightened psychological risk for girls. Girls at this time have been observed to lose their vitality, their resilience, their immunity to depression, their sense of themselves, and their character." During a season of life when we needed daily encouragement to deepen our relationship to our natural vitality, resilience, immunity to depression, and sense of self, we were encouraged to be other-focused, other-directed, and other-involved. We were taught and, sadly, we teach our daughters, ineffective behaviors that further alienate us from ourselves.

The Vow-Composition Process

Inspired by the stories of the women with whom I have worked and incorporating the insights of my own journey home, I developed the "Vow of Faithfulness" composition process by refashioning the wedding vow and wedding ceremony into transformational resources for women. There are four purposes for this universally understood and powerfully experienced process.

1. The first purpose is to reverse our socialization by reminding us of the way home to ourselves. This intention is informed by an understanding of the following three ineffective, yet culturally mandated, behaviors for girls and women:

∽ *Overresponsibility:* The girl-child is encouraged to get caught up in the actions, thoughts, feelings, and journeys of others. As a result, she assumes inappropriate responsibility for the cause, modification, and outcome of the choices, behaviors, and actions of others. Distracted, we lose touch with our own lives. In the fullness of time, we become dizzy from swirling in the lives of others. We become willing to journey home to ourselves. The vow-composition process supports us to take full responsibility for the cause, modification, and outcome of the *our own* choices, behaviors, and actions.

∽ *People Pleasing:* The girl-child is encouraged to shape her body, thoughts, feelings, behaviors, and relationships according to the specifications of others. As a result, she develops a crippling oversensitivity to and dependence on the opinions of others. Twisted out of shape, she loses touch with her inner resources of wisdom and creativity. In the fullness of time, our bodies, thoughts, feelings, and relationships ache for their true expression. We become willing to journey home to ourselves. The vow-composition process supports us to design our own lives, discover our own feelings and thoughts, embrace our woman-bodies, and conceive of relationships that work for us.

Twisted into the shapes of experts, of family expectations, of job descriptions,

We lose touch with our feelings, our thoughts, and the shape-spinning center within us.

All who are aching, come. Courage awaits you here. Rediscover the shape of your life.

—PLR

∽ *Overinvolvement:* The girl-child is groomed to be a caretaker. She will be expected to anticipate and then meet the emotional and physical needs of others. As a result, she becomes preoccupied with servicing others with her energy, attention, and creativity. Depleted, we lose touch with our own needs and desires. In the fullness of time, our resources become depleted from servicing others with our attention, energy, and creativity. We become willing to journey home to ourselves. The vow-composition process supports us to reclaim our personal resources, to meet our own emotional and physical needs, and to conceive of relationships of reciprocity.

2. The second purpose of the vow-composition process is to support us to grow in knowledge and love of ourselves. As we journey home, we discover untapped resources and unused capacities. It is essential to reclaim these resources and capacities—they are our birthright as children of life. The vow-composition process supports us to befriend the richness within us. As we reclaim our natural resources and capacities, we redirect our life energy away from the "swirling" patterns of old toward adventures of self-discovery. No longer denying any aspect of ourselves, we tap into our own self-healing capacities as deeper layers of inner truth and wisdom became available to us. We grow in knowledge and love of ourselves.

From birth, you possess three natural resources: your breath, your woman-body, and your inner life. They are faithful escorts on your journey home. The vow-composition process outlined in chapter 6 will support you in reclaiming these essential resources.

Servicing others with our energy, creativity, and life,

We lose touch with our needs, our desires, and the replenishing center within us.

All who are depleted, come.
Wisdom awaits you here.
Rediscover compassionate connection.
—PLR

Your birthright also includes eight natural capacities which will be explored in chapter 7. They are the capacity to live in your body fully and completely; the capacity to express and meet your body's organic needs; the capacity to meet your own sexual needs; the capacity to recognize and express your feelings; the capacity to trust your own perceptions and to tell the truth; the capacity to sustain interest in yourself and involvement in your own pursuits; the capacity to create from your own unique vision of the world; and the capacity to celebrate yourself, welcoming recognition and acknowledgment. As you reclaim your organic resources and capacities, the composition of your own vow of faithfulness will flow gracefully and naturally from your deepening self-knowledge and love.

3. The third purpose is to prepare us for healthy relationships with others. These insights support the third intention:

∞ Our capacity to be available to others is in direct proportion to how substantially we are available to ourselves. The vow-composition process invites you to turn toward yourself with interest and attention; to acknowledge your own feelings, thoughts, and perceptions; and to offer yourself support through life's challenges and celebrations. In this way, your capacity to be available to others will deepen.

∞ Our capacity to live nonjudgmentally is in direct proportion to how deeply we have accepted ourselves. The vow-composition process invites you to descend into your own richly textured humanity in all its trouble and beauty, gift and challenge, awkwardness and

Transformation comes from looking deep within, to a state that exists before fear and isolation arise, the state in which we are inviolably whole just as we are. We connect to ourselves, to our own true experience, and discover there that to be alive means to be whole.
—SHARON SALZBERG

grace, turning a merciful eye toward all that you discover. In this way, your capacity to live compassionately will deepen.

∾ Our capacity to love others is in direct proportion to how deeply we love ourselves. The vow-composition process invites you to gaze upon your past and present, your body and its needs, your ideas and emotions, your resources and capacities, your injury and exquisite potential with loving kindness. In this way, your capacity to love will deepen.

∾ Our capacity to participate in our relationships is in direct proportion to how fully we have participated in our lives. The vow-composition process invites you to participate in your own life, meeting each challenge with creativity, and taking action on your own behalf with clarity and strength. In this way, your capacity to participate meaningfully in your significant relationships will deepen.

∾ Our capacity to remain faithful to another is in direct proportion to the depth of our loyalty to ourselves. The vow-composition process invites you to maintain loyalty to yourself through all the seasons of life, to preserve allegiance to yourself even in the face of opposition. In this way, your capacity to sustain interest in others and to remain faithful to them will deepen.

Most fundamentally, the vow composition process invites you to turn inward and reestablish the relationship to yourself that most of us lost on

The person whose self is thwarted can only love in an ambivalent way; that is with the strong part of her self she can love, with the crippled part she must hate.
—ERICH FROMM,
SELFISHNESS AND SELF-LOVE

> *We often look elsewhere for what we already possess; we project. We turn to others to give us a level of acceptance we can only give to ourselves. Every time we reclaim some of our own energies and stop projecting onto others attributes of ourselves, we become more whole, more present.*
> —MARION WOODMAN, *COMING HOME TO MYSELF*

our way through adolescence. By accepting the invitation, you offer yourself what was needed most in childhood and adolescence: support to go on a remarkable adventure of self-discovery, deepening your relationship to your vitality, resilience, and sense of self. Years ago, I chose the calla lily as the logo for the "vow of faithfulness" process. In a time when God was imagined as woman, the lily represented the Goddess' self-fertilization powers. The solitary calla lily stands self-possessed and powerful, full of beauty and grace, encouraging you to return home to yourself, to grow in knowledge and love of yourself, and to vow faithfulness to your natural resources and capacities.

The Essential Vow of Faithfulness

A vow of faithfulness is a sacred assertion, a positive declaration, affirmation, or statement, expressing a woman's intention to remain loyal to herself, to preserve allegiance to herself even when challenged and opposed. Self-love is moody. Much like our love for the significant others in our lives, its intensity ebbs and flows. Writing a formal vow reminds us of the truth about ourselves when we forget. It re-centers us when challenged by the ingrained habits of overresponsibility, people pleasing, and overinvolvement. It reminds us of the way home when we wander away from what is truest

> *Women have to understand that regardless of who does not want us we have to want ourselves. Self-love is the first and hardest rule to stick by. Women need to not abandon themselves in their quest for bliss and love. You can love yourself spiritually, physically, in almost any way anybody else can.*
> —ALICE WALKER, *MS MAGAZINE*

and best for us, when we become distracted from our primary relationship—
to ourselves.

There is no "right" way to compose an essential vow. Consider the following vows, representing each of the three purposes of the vow-composition
process. I encourage *all women* to personalize them as they journey home to
themselves. Highlight the phrases that resonate with your own experience. By
the end of the chapter, you may have composed your first formal vow of faithfulness to yourself.

Recognizing the tenacity of my socialization, I vow to actively reverse
its repercussions in my life and relationships:

I am dizzy from swirling in the lives of others. I am willing to
journey home to myself. I vow to develop the capacity to take full
responsibility for the cause, modification, and outcome of my own
choices, behaviors, and actions.

My body, thoughts, feelings, and relationships ache for their true
expression. I am willing to journey home to myself. I vow to develop the capacity to design my own life, discover my own feelings and thoughts, embrace my woman-body, and conceive of relationships that work for me. I will learn to please myself.

My resources are depleted from servicing others with my attention, energy, and creativity. I am willing to journey home to myself. I vow to reclaim my personal resources and develop the

As one respects oneself so one can respect others. That is one of the peculiarities of human personality that can always be depended on. If there is a valid and real attitude toward the self, that attitude will be manifested as valid and real toward others. It is not that as you judge so shall you be judged, but as you judge yourself so shall you judge others.
—Harry Stack Sullivan,
Conceptions of Modern Psychiatry

capacity to meet my own emotional and physical needs and to conceive of relationships of reciprocity.

As I grow in knowledge and love of myself, I am reclaiming my untapped resources and unused capacities:

I vow to love my body all the days of my life, supporting it with strength; to listen to the deep wisdom of my body, meeting its needs with tenderness and grace; to embrace my sexuality and explore the edges of my sensuality; to honor the whole range of human emotion, allowing each feeling to pass through me as gracefully as a breath; to speak my truth, refusing to defer to the thoughts and perceptions of others; to sustain interest in myself, embracing my own life as teacher, healer, and challenge; to celebrate my unique vision and experience, refusing to color inside someone else's lines; to be full of myself, honoring my desire for acknowledgment and recognition.

Recognizing that my relationships with others mirror my relationship with myself:

I vow to turn toward myself with interest and attention to acknowledge my own feelings, thoughts, and perceptions, and to offer myself support through life's challenges and celebrations. I will cultivate my availability to myself and, without effort, my capacity to be available to others will deepen.

I vow to descend into my own richly textured humanity in all its trouble and beauty, gift and challenge, awkwardness and grace, turning a mer-

28

> *Loving yourself . . . does not mean being self-absorbed or narcissistic, or disregarding others. Rather it means welcoming yourself as the most honored guest in your own heart, a guest worthy of respect, a lovable companion.*
> —Margo Anand,
> *The Art of Sexual Ecstasy*

ciful eye toward all that I discover. I will cultivate compassion toward myself and, without effort, my capacity to live compassionately will deepen.

I vow to gaze upon my past and present, my body and its needs, my ideas and emotions, my resources and capacities, and my injury and exquisite potential with loving kindness. I will cultivate self-love and, without effort, my capacity to love others will deepen.

I vow to participate in my own life, meeting each challenge with creativity, and taking action on my own behalf with clarity and strength. As I do, my capacity to participate meaningfully in my significant relationships will deepen.

I vow to maintain loyalty to myself through all the seasons of life and to preserve allegiance to myself even in the face of opposition. As I do, my capacity to sustain interest in others and to remain faithful to them will deepen.

The Ceremony of Commitment

The "vow of faithfulness" retreats I facilitate culminate with a Ceremony of Commitment in which each woman's essential vow is witnessed by the gathered community. Using the main features of a traditional wedding liturgy, I refashioned the wedding ceremony into a transformational resource for women. The ceremony provides an opportunity for

There is a vitality, a life force, a quickening, that is translated through you into action. And because there is only one of you in all time, this expression is unique. And if you block it, it will never exist through any other medium and it will be lost. The world will not have it. It is not your business to determine how good it is, nor how valuable, nor how it compares to other expressions. It is your business to keep it yours clearly and directly. To keep the channel open.
—MARTHA GRAHAM

30

Life is swift and precious while it's in our grasp. Loving yourself is such a small act of appreciation for the everlasting Love that has breathed you into being and on whose wings you will be carried when it's time to leave this life.

—PAULA M. REEVES,
WOMEN'S INTUITION

women to make their self-love public. It also gathers together a community of support, both to witness each woman's vow and to hold her accountable to her truest intentions. In this chapter I focus on the retreat or basic ceremony. Subsequent chapters, however, contain a variety of other ceremonies. Some women integrate the reading of their vows into already established rituals: birthdays, bridal and mother-to-be showers, graduation parties, therapy sessions, women's circles, and support groups. Others create personalized ceremonies based on their own religious backgrounds or on current spiritual paths.

To create the basic ceremony, I incorporated eight components of the traditional wedding ceremony. They are the call to gather, the invocation, musical interludes and readings, the commitments, the vows, the blessing and reception of the symbol, the pronouncement of loving partnership, and the closing blessing. Each component has a particular purpose:

1. *The Call to Gather:* Usually spoken by the officiate, this statement invites your guests to be present by shifting their focus from the busyness of their day and lives to the sacredness of this moment. It states the reason for which you are gathered.

Any ritual is an opportunity for transformation. To do ritual, you must be willing to be transformed in some way. That inner willingness is what makes the ritual come alive and have power.

—STARHAWK

2. *The Invocation:* This prayer invites the God of your understanding to be present. It enlarges the circle to include the sacred. Some folks invite the God of traditional religion to be present; others invoke the Goddess, the natural world, the ancestors, or the silence.

3. *Music and Readings:* Interspersed throughout the ceremony are songs and readings that support your growing self-knowledge, self-acceptance, self-love, and self-commitment—songs and readings that invite you home to yourself. Appropriate quotations and readings fill the margins of this book and, most likely, your journals.

4. *The Commitments:* Using the eight elements of my first personal vow (pages 12–14), I refashioned the traditional "I Will" questions into a set of foundational self-affirming commitments. In response, women respond, "I Will."

5. *The Vows:* Here the vows are spoken or read. Here each woman's self-love is made public to be acknowledged, supported, celebrated, and emulated. The gathered community is invited to review their self-commitments as they listen.

6. *The Blessing and Reception of the Symbol:* In preparation for the ceremony, each woman chooses a symbolic item, such as a ring, earring, stone, feather, or scarf, as a tangible reminder of her vow. During this part of the ceremony, the symbolic item is blessed and returned to her.

7. *The Pronouncement of Loving Partnership:* The officiant makes this public proclamation that you have turned toward yourself to establish a lifelong partnership of love, respect, and loyalty.

8. *The Closing Blessing:* Traditionally spoken by the officiant, the closing blessing sends us on our way with good wishes, open hearts, and buoyed spirits. In the refashioned ceremony, each participate boldly blesses herself with a chant-affirmation, affirming "This is it. This is my life. . . ."

The "Ceremony of Commitment" was intended for use in a forest setting and reflects the insights of a woman-affirming spirituality. If you choose to use this ceremony, personalize the script to reflect the natural setting of your choice and the spiritual metaphors in harmony with your own beliefs. Invite your closest friend, or a therapist, minister, or rabbi to officiate.

The Ceremony of Commitment in the Redwood Circle
A CALL TO GATHER

(Personalize to reflect natural setting of your choice.)

Open your eyes and look around you.
We have chosen the forest as our cathedral.
We have invited the tall ancient redwoods as honored guests.
We have invited the inhabitants of the forest to be among us.
We have invited the moist, green growing things to bless us.
We have gathered to witness each woman's vow of faithfulness to herself.
Be present in this place.

Open your heart and look within you.
Breathe into this moment and release all distractions,
Excursions into the past, projections into the future.
Breathing in, receive the fullness of this moment.
Breathing out, open your heart to the gift and challenge of this moment.
We are gathered to witness each woman's vow of faithfulness to herself.
Be present here and now.

AN INVOCATION OF SPIRIT

(Personalize to reflect the spiritual metaphors in harmony with your
own beliefs.)

We invoke the presence of the Source of All Life.
Everything in the forest comes from and returns to the Mother.
You are as grounded, as connected to Her as the trees are.
You are held, supported, and nourished by Her.
Acknowledge the firm ground of the Mother, holding you.
Mother, we welcome you here.

We invoke the spirit of life, the breath.
Everything breathes in the forest.
Savor the breath of life, flowing in, through, and around you.
Inhale deeply as the breath rises from the rich earth beneath you.
Release the breath into the cool moist air around you.
Breath, we welcome you here.

We invoke the wisdom of the body.
Notice the ancient trees around you. You are one with the forest.
Feel your feet grow roots extending deep into the ground.
Feel your arms become branches stretching high in the sky.
Sway with the breeze. Settle into your woman-body.
Wise body, we welcome you here.

We invoke the accumulation of our years and experience.
Notice the forest-dance of life and death and rebirth.
Reach down and touch the forest floor, layered with seasons passed.
Look up and view the forest canopy woven from time's evolving.

Acknowledge the seasons of your life. Invoke the richness of your years.
Accumulation of years and experience, we welcome you here.

MUSICAL INTERLUDE

A COMMITMENT

(Personalize the questions to reflect your own self-affirming perspective.)

Daughter of Woman, in response to the truth, in love with yourself,
Full of boldness and grace, express your commitment with the words
"I Will."

Will you love your body all the days of your life?
Will you touch it with tenderness and support it with strength?
Will you honor its rhythms and cycles as an exquisite resource?
Will you honor the body of the goddess in your changing body?

Will you listen to the deep wisdom of your body all the days of your life?
Will you meet its needs with tenderness and grace?
Will you design the shape of your days in accordance with its feedback?
Will you eat foods that support its vitality, drink water to moisten its
    capacities, and sleep well to renew its life energy?

Will you embrace your sexuality as your own all the days of your life?
Will you delight in pleasuring yourself?
Will you explore the edges of your sensuality?
Will you trust your body's clear "Yes" and "No" in the choice of lovers?

Will you honor the whole range of human emotion all the days of
    your life?

34

Will you circulate your feelings daily, using sound, movement, and image,
    allowing them to pass through you as gracefully as the breath?
Will you take responsibility for meeting your own emotional needs,
    enlisting the support of respectful friends and chosen family?

Will you speak your truth all the days of your life?
Will you tell the untold truths of a lifetime to your parents, lovers, and
    colleagues, and to your children and grandchildren?
Will you assume intellectual equality by refusing to defer to the thoughts
    and perceptions of others?

Will you love your creative impulses all the days of your life?
Will you give expression daily to the words, shapes, images, and move-
    ments that emerge from within you?
Will you celebrate your unique vision and experience, producing original
    creations and refusing to color inside someone else's lines?

Will you sustain interest in yourself all the days of your life?
Will you embrace your own life as teacher, healer, and challenge?
Will you value its lessons above the prescriptions of experts?
Will you befriend the solitude of your own life?

Will you choose to be full of yourself all the days of your life?
Will you honor your desire for acknowledgment and recognition?
Will you surround yourself with friends who applaud your fullness?

MUSICAL INTERLUDE
READING OF THE VOWS

To be said before the women speak:

"Let us witness each woman's vow of faithfulness.

Let us review our commitment to ourselves as we listen."

Each woman speaks her vow.

BLESSING OF THE SYMBOLS

Spoken to bless the symbols:

"With holy water from the womb of the Mother, we bless each symbol.

May it be a reminder of your vow when you forget yourself.

May it escort you home when you wander away from yourself.

May it bring a smile to your soul all the days of your life."

To be said as call and response after all women have received their symbols:

"As a sign of my love and respect for myself," (Women repeat)

"I give myself this ___ with a pledge to honor my vow" (Repeat)

"In tender times and turbulent times" (Repeat)

"In graceful moments and in awkward situations" (Repeat)

"In flowing times and in seasons of stagnation" (Repeat)

"In fullness and in emptiness" (Repeat)

"In fear and in courage" (Repeat)

"In trouble and in beauty" (Repeat)

"With all that I am and all I shall become" (Repeat)

"For the rest of my life." (Repeat)

To be said by the gathered community: "So be it."

A Pronouncement of Loving Partnership

Inasmuch as you,_____, have grown in knowledge and love of yourself, and have vowed faithfulness to your own life and capacities, I now joyfully proclaim that it is right and good that you are woman. You are full of yourself!

A Blessing

To be said by all participants in unison:

"No More Waiting.
This is it.
This is my life.
Nothing to wait for.
Nowhere else to go.
No one to make it all different.
This is it.
What a relief to have finally landed
Here . . . now.
Blessed be my life!"

THREE

Remaining Loyal to Yourself:
Composing Companion Vows for All
Seasons of Life

Daughter of woman, honor your vow in tender times and turbulent times. In graceful moments and in awkward situations. In flowing times and in seasons of stagnation. In fullness and in emptiness. In fear and in courage. In trouble and in beauty. With all that you are and all you shall become. For the rest of your life.

nce we have reestablished our primary relationship with ourselves through the composition of the "essential vow of faithfulness" discussed in chapter 2, the vow-composition process can be used to support us through all of life's crises, challenges, and celebrations because of the universality of its form and the intuitive wisdom of its content. Over the years, the vows I have helped women to compose have fallen into five categories: circumstantial, retrospective, preparatory, supportive, and transformational. The composition of any or all of these vows may be useful to you depending on where you are in your life.

A Seasonal Resource

The circumstantial and retrospective vows are grounded in the ongoing details and regular rhythm of life. They invite us to "flesh out" our essential vow—our intention to remain loyal to ourselves—in the nitty-gritty of life. They will be described generally so you can decide if and when they may be appropriate for you or someone you know.

1. *Circumstantial vows* are motivated by a particular circumstance and its time-specific challenges.

    ∞ Elsie decided to spend the summer traveling alone throughout Europe. Although excited, she was aware of the challenges of traveling alone as a woman. She gathered friends together to share their travel insights and experiences which she then wove into her "vow of faithfulness." Her vow began, "While traveling through Europe, I will not engage in sex with strangers. I will trust my intuition in every situation and if I feel I am in any danger, no matter the appearances, I will leave. I will check in with my family every other day." Elsie consulted her vow daily. It reminded her of her inner home when she lost her bearings and of her community of supportive friends when she felt lonely or anxious.

∞ Sharon planned to spend a week with her parents. Aware of the historic challenges extended visits posed, she composed a vow specific to the visit with help from her therapist and a close friend. It began, "I will stay at a bed-and-breakfast rather than at my parent's home. I will consult my parents about their availability during my stay. I will spend time with them within a broader itinerary that includes visits with old friends, exploration of the community, and alone time with my favorite book and journal." Sharon reviewed her vow daily. It supported her to keep her boundaries clear and to honor her primary relationship to herself.

Is there a particular circumstance you want to infuse with consciousness by composing a vow of faithfulness to yourself? Share the nature of the circumstance and its inherent challenges with a circle of your friends and supporters. Weave their insight, wisdom, and experience into a vow of faithfulness. Consult it regularly to prepare for the circumstance.

2. *Retrospective vows* are motivated by the desire to review one's life, usually on a birthday. For example: Carmen was approaching her sixtieth birthday. She wanted to review the six decades of her life to acknowledge the lessons of self-discovery and to create a special celebration for her birthday. Carmen spent three months reviewing each decade, recording insights gained and lessons learned. She wove each insight and lesson into her vow. She read it to her family and friends at her sixtieth birthday party. It began, "My life has been my teacher. May I always honor its lessons above the prescriptions of experts, the expectations of the culture, and the exhortations of religious doctrines and creeds."

In preparation for your next birthday, gather the accumulation of your years and experience by incorporating your lifetime's worth of insight and self-discovery into an evolving vow of faithfulness. Review and renew it on each subsequent birthday.

An Evolving Resource

Preparatory vows encourage women who are about to enter marriage or begin parenting to "remember themselves."*Supportive vows* help women in transition to stay firmly grounded in the present moment as they "gather the gifts" of the past to bring with them into the future. Transformative vows invite women to "discover the way home" to their natural resources and to "descend into the richness" of their natural capacities. Over the years, the composition of these vows has evolved into four separate processes:

1. Remembering Yourself: Composing a Vow to Prepare for Marriage and/or the Birth of a Child

2. Gathering the Gifts: Composing a Vow to Support Conscious Endings and New Beginnings

3. Discovering the Way Home: Composing a Vow to Reclaim Your Natural Resources

4. Descending into the Richness: Composing a Vow to Reclaim Your Natural Capacities

In this chapter I outline the evolution of these four processes. Subsequently, each process has its own chapter and that chapter provides step-by-step guidance for composing a vow and creating a ceremony. To inspire you, I have included the stories of women who have worked through the processes. Continue to highlight the words and phrases that resonate with your own experience. Consciously or under the ground of your consciousness, you are composing a vow of faithfulness as you read through the book.

Remembering Yourself: Composing a Vow to Prepare for Marriage and/or the Birth of a Child

Couples often request my assistance in planning and facilitating their wedding ceremonies. Nathan and Sandy were a conscious couple who had the necessary skills to celebrate the gifts and to navigate the challenges of their partnership. When it was time for us to design the ceremony and for them to write their vows, Sandy phoned me. She felt blocked and hadn't begun her vow to Nathan. She was in conflict because the romantic, idealistic vows so often said at weddings didn't fit for her. She wanted to preface her commitment to

Nathan with a clear commitment to herself. I encouraged Sandy to trust her intuition and to spend the time writing a vow to herself. She phoned me a week later to report that when she completed her vow to herself, her vow to Nathan flowed without effort.

Inspired by Sandy's experience, I developed the "Remembering Yourself" process for engaged women who fear losing themselves in their partners' lives, being swallowed up by the demands of marriage, and being distracted from their own projects and dreams by the expectations of marriage. Many of them watched their quintessentially female mothers ignore their creativity and vocational interests, set aside their projects and dreams, and postpone completing degrees in order to finance the dreams of others with their blood, sweat, and tears. One woman lamented, "My fear is that it's in the genes. No matter how much hard work I do to counter the habitual loss-of-self-once-married syndrome, my partner and I will revert to the way marriage has always been done. I hope the process of composing a vow to myself will change my negative thinking and support me to remain loyal to myself in the marriage."

Most women want to find the middle space in which it is possible to honor their own needs, interests, and projects, and to be significantly involved with a partner. Filled with a mixture of fear, hope, and excitement, they work through the process. It does indeed relieve their anxiety, support their hope, and provide an outlet for their excitement. As engaged women compose vows of faithfulness to themselves, they review the navigational tools necessary to return "home" if they wander away from themselves. Acknowledging that distractions are a

44

reality of life, they embrace the life practice of noticing distraction without judgment and then returning, always returning home to themselves.

To culminate the "Remembering Yourself" process, some women create a ceremony to which they invite their closest friends and allies. Others choose to read their vows at the bridal shower or rehearsal dinner. Whatever the chosen format, women pledge to honor their vows in tender times and turbulent times, in graceful moments and in awkward situations, in flowing times and in seasons of stagnation, in fullness and in emptiness, in fear and in courage, and in trouble and in beauty. They review their vows monthly and renew them yearly. When faced with marital challenges, they review their vows before confronting their partners. For all of us, regular cultivation of the partnership with ourselves is the best investment we can make in our significant relationships.

Over the years I have adapted the "Remembering Yourself" process for mothers and mothers-to-be. The prospect of parenting brings up a similar set of fears as those described by engaged women: fear of losing oneself, fear of being consumed by the other. Moms wonder, "Will I lose myself in the swirls of parenting? Where will I find the stamina, courage, and inner strength to sustain my commitment to the child?" Women set aside fifteen minutes a day during pregnancy or prior to the coming of their adoptive child to work through the vow-composition process, incorporating the lessons of their own lives, the wisdom and experience of other mothers, and a commitment to continue setting aside fifteen minutes a

45

> It is easy to become so immersed in motherhood and its responsibilities that a woman's total identity is MOM. Her interests and hobbies and other things that nurture her get shelved. She gives and gives, and suddenly wakes up depressed and wonders why. Why? She's neglected the things that feed her soul. . . . If a woman is nurturing herself—not as a mom, but as a person—she has a more balanced identity. Therefore her mothering will come more from a place of power because she will be happier.
>
> —ANDREA ALBAN GOSLINE,
> MOTHER'S NATURE

day to "remember herself." When the vow is complete, the mother creates a ceremony to which she invites her family and friends or she chooses to read her vow at the baby shower. Over time she experiences the benefits of regularly cultivating the partnership with herself—again, it's the most effective investment she can make in her growing family.

SANDY: "I prefaced my vow to my husband with a vow of faithfulness to myself. Reading my vow during the ceremony rounded out the experience for me. My wedding wasn't just an event in which I was getting married to a man—it was my life taking its next right step. It became a part of the circle of my life, rather than an isolated commitment to a man. It felt complete."

JESSICA: "Pregnancy was the perfect time to write a vow to myself. I was moving from one season of life to another and wanted to do it with consciousness. I set aside fifteen minutes a day for myself. The habit of 'remembering myself' has stuck. I continue to cherish 'my time' each day even as I care for our newborn. The vow reminds me that I can't be there for my family unless I'm available to myself."

PATRICIA: "I vow faithfulness to myself within my significant relationship. I will be faithful to my need for solitude between times of closeness with my beloved: to integrate the experiences of our rich intimacy, to return home to

Pregnancy is a natural time to begin or deepen the practice of mindfulness. The increasingly dramatic changes that occur in our bodies and in our very perceptions, thoughts, and emotions invite new degrees of wakefulness, wonder, and appreciation. For some of us, being pregnant may be the first time we experience being fully in our bodies.
—MYLA AND JON KABAT-ZINN, *EVERYDAY BLESSINGS*

myself, and to breathe into my being the healing, challenge, and comfort of our closeness. I will be faithful to my beloved friends and chosen family, incorporating regular times with them into my life. I will be faithful to my need for three days of complete surrender to my creative process: to follow its impulses, to nurture the business that sustains it, and to cultivate an audience to receive the fruit of my creative endeavors. I will be faithful to my need to sleep alone several nights a week and to wake up in my own bed on the days I choose for creative focus."

Gathering the Gifts: Composing a Vow to Support Conscious Endings and New Beginnings

The week after I began writing my first book, I sat at the computer unable to work. Rather than berate myself, I listened to the resistant part of me. An anxious voice emerged. Through a written dialogue with "The Anxious One," it became clear that the level of focus and attention required of the writing project was overwhelming me. I asked the Anxious One how I might support her. I began setting up "pillows of support" around my life in order to go the distance with the creative project.

My first commitment was to weekly bodywork. I wrote a check for the first month's sessions to assure the anxious part of me that I was serious about attending to my body's needs. Each day I checked in with the Anxious One, "Now may I go back to

My current view of the world is that life is braided streams of light and darkness, joy and pain, and I just accept them. They both exist and I walk them both. But now I know there is a choice about what I do about them. This awareness is one of the delights of being forty.
—ARISIKA RAZAK,
  ON WOMEN TURNING FORTY

work?" "No," was the clear response. The second pillow of support was weekly attendance at a writers' group. We offered each other ongoing encouragement and feedback. I checked in again—still not enough support.

My third pillow was two full days off every week as a reminder that life was wider than the writing project. As I assembled this rich assortment of pillows, the anxious part of me relaxed. Three weeks later, having renewed my vow to listen to the deep wisdom of my own life, to meet its needs with tenderness and grace, and to design my days in accordance with its feedback, I returned to my writing tasks without effort.

When we *panic* in response to the challenges of life, we are prone to second-guess our impulses, to pathologize our decisions, to theorize about our feelings, and to endlessly process and complain about our lives and relationships. Based on our earliest socialization, we long for a savior to come along and fix the situation for us. When this dependency-based response to life and its challenges becomes habitual, our creative resources lay dormant within us. On the other hand, when we *participate* in the challenges of life, we take responsibility for our decisions, feel our feelings, actively engage our lives and relationships, and celebrate our own stunning capacities as children of life. Our creative capacities rise to meet the challenge and we take action on our own behalf with clarity and strength.

Based on the distinction between panic and participation, I developed the "Gathering the Gifts" vow-composition process. The process has been especially helpful to women during transitional moments when they are in that in-between life space—neither here nor there—stepping into the unknown as they begin a new life situation or leave a career, relationship, way of life, or self-understanding. Some transitions have a hard edge—they are thrust upon us without our consent. It's easy to panic when all the "neatness," predictability, and security of our lives, relationships, or health have shattered into a hundred pieces and now lay in a chaotic mess at our feet due to an unexpected diagnosis or the sudden loss of a job or loved one. Other transitions are chosen: folks choose to leave good jobs for even better ones, to bring closure to effective therapeutic relationships, or to move beyond no-longer-working friendships or partnerships. Still other transitions, like graduation from high school, college, or graduate school, are part of the benevolent flow of life. When we're moving from one situation to another due to circumstance or choice, we can lose our balance.

No matter the type of transition, the "Gathering the Gifts" vow-composition process provides the grounding necessary to create safe passage through transitional seasons of life. Refusing to entertain the question, "Who will save me?", the process supports women in transition to create strategies to address life challenges. It will encourage you to tap into your own resources of creativity and wisdom and to gather pillows of support to accompany you through challenging times. Incorporating the lessons of the past and the possibilities of the future while firmly grounded in the present moment, your vow becomes your north star, your guiding light, the faithful breath you return to in the midst of the "creative chaos" of transition. The vow supports you to embrace your own life, valuing its lessons above the prescriptions of experts, and to participate fully in the challenges of life, using them as opportunities to sharpen your skills for conscious living and to deepen your partnership with yourself.

> HELEN: "I was married at eighteen and spent the next forty years
> supporting my husband's career. He died unexpectedly. While
> writing my vow of faithfulness during the transitional period after

his death, I remembered my own dream of becoming a pediatric nurse and vowed to fulfill it."

SUSAN: "It was time to say good-bye to my therapist of five years. I was ready to move on. I wanted to infuse this transition with consciousness because it represented a major milestone in my life. With my therapist's support, I had grown to trust myself. I read through the five journals that represented five years' worth of inward exploration and self-discovery. I incorporated each insight into my first vow of faithfulness. I will read my vow to my therapist during a final get-together in my art studio."

Discovering the Way Home: Composing a Vow to Reclaim Your Natural Resources

In the very beginning of her life, the girl-child is acquainted with the exquisite natural resources of her breath, body, and inner life. She breathes deeply into her belly. She loves her body. She is in touch with the wisdom within her own life. Over time, however, the girl-child becomes disconnected from "home." She becomes outer-directed and loses touch with herself. Her breath becomes shallow. She ignores her body. She looks to "saviors" outside of herself for salvation and validation, forgetting the rich resources within her. Estranged from her own life, she becomes susceptible to the swirls of others.

Women's "swirls" range from pleasing boyfriends to rescuing alcoholic children, from supporting husbands' careers to meeting the body-beautiful demands of the culture, and from searching for the "perfect" self-improvement regimen to fulfilling the expectations of New Age gurus. Sadly, these swirls require disengagement from our bodies: we ignore our organic needs for food, rest, orgasm, exercise, elimination, and touch; from our breath: being out of breath with no time to "catch our breath" is the norm; and from our inner life: there's no time to check in with our own wisdom and resources. We swirl until we lose our breath and bearings, until we become dizzy.

In the fullness of time, motivated by our dizziness, many of us reach out to a counselor, spiritual community, or self-help group. We are offered information, insight, and tools of support. We are inspired by the experience, strength, and hope of others who are detaching from the swirls of others and turning toward their own lives. Many of us spend years of our lives in therapy, recovery, or spirituality circles, however, continuing our disempowering dependence on "powers" outside of ourselves to legitimize, direct, and save us. In the process, we become more deeply alienated from our own inner resources.

Truly woman-affirming therapeutic, spirituality, or personal growth programs must offer us more than insight, information, and camaraderie. They must facilitate reconnection to our natural resources: breath, woman-body, and inner life. Based on this conviction, I developed the "Home Is Always Waiting" meditation, which is the centerpiece of the "Discovering the Way Home" vow-composition process. It begins with these words: "Home is always waiting. It is as near as a conscious breath, conscious contact with your woman-body, and a descent into the rich resources of your inner life." This process supports daily contact with our natural resources. We can rediscover the way home—the path is as near as a conscious breath, conscious contact with our woman-body, and a descent into the richness of our inner life.

As we discover the way home to a deep breath, our original body-centeredness is reestablished. With each breath, we actively nourish the body, balance its systems, listen to the wisdom of its sensations, and participate fully in every body-centered activity. As we turn our attention inward, we reverse the lifelong habit of focusing outside of ourselves. As we gather ourselves and what is nourishing on the inhalation, and then release our sense of responsibility for the lives of others on the exhalation, we participate in an organic rhythm that supports health on every level of our being. Conscious breathing supports us to pause in the midst of our busy lives to pay attention to our bodily sensations. They are the voice of their organic needs for food, rest, orgasm, exercise, elimination, and touch. With each deep breath, we become more skillful at discerning the intention and wisdom of bodily sensations. As we step into self-responsibility, we meet the needs of our bodies with tenderness and grace.

A woman's body is an essential resource on the way home to herself. Initially we are uncomfortable turning toward our bodies with tenderness and conscious, prolonged attention. Our discomfort makes great sense. Most of us have developed a chronic resentment toward our bodies because they are always falling short of perfection as defined by the culture, our families, a current lover, and ourselves. They are never quite good enough no matter what we do to them. The "Discovering Your Way Home" process invites us to notice our discomfort without judgment, and then imagine it riding on the back of the breath to be released with each exhalation. As we turn a merciful eye toward our bodies, we reverse our harsh scrutiny and chronic resentment of them. We come home to our bodies as they are and commit the forbidden act, the essential political act, of loving our bodies as we

Daring to breathe is actually daring to live. As we all know, when we cease breathing, we die. As long as we are alive, the depth of our breathing determines the amount of life force we bring into ourselves. Given only a stingy amount of oxygen, our bodies, hearts, and minds will not function well.
—SUE PATTON THOELE,
THE WOMAN'S BOOK OF SOUL

did in the very beginning of our lives. With each loving touch, we honor the body as the sacred temple of the spirit of life. We embrace it as a community of support within us, a harmonious partnership of cells, tissues, organs, and systems. We enter into a partnership with our bodies, improving conscious contact with them through meditation, and consulting them through each season of her life. We celebrate our bodies as exquisite resources, faithful allies, and trustworthy companions. We pay attention to the body's sensations as faithful reminders of the way home.

When we swirl outward, we are thrown off balance. When we spiral inward, we are drawn toward our center and we rest. The "Discovering the Way Home" process invites us to turn inward. Instead of ascending to enlightened states of being that involve the denial of the self, we discover that ours is a journey of descent—we look deep within to reclaim forgotten aspects of ourselves. We reach beneath our obsession with flaws, beneath the accomplishments that mask our sense of unworthiness, beneath years of alienation from ourselves, toward the goodness at our center. We discover that the good is deeply embedded within us. As we embrace our original goodness, our inner spaces are cleared out and reclaimed as our own. We find rest within our own lives and accept all of ourselves as worthy.

The "Returning Home" process begins with a simple breath and concludes with the composition of a vow of faithfulness As we return home to ourselves, we do not have the time or energy to get caught up in the swirls of others. Whenever we are tempted to allow anything to become the controlling or organizing focus of our time, energy, and attention, we choose to focus on the creative projects, life concerns, and personal challenges that clamor for our attention. Within our vow, we express our commitment to least three creative projects, life concerns, and personal challenges. The "Home Is Always

Waiting" meditation and our list of personal commitments escort us home when we wander away from ourselves. They support us to remain loyal to ourselves. Regardless.

JEN: "I am learning how to breathe for the first time in my forty years. I am becoming one with my breath through a regular practice of meditation inspired by the "Discovering the Way Home" vow-composition process. Through meditation, I can touch the core of myself, the center where my Deeper Wisdom dwells. The breath teaches me to trust my inner resources."

LANA: "Supported by my vow of faithfulness, I am more conscious of myself. My armor is melting. Deeper layers of inner truth are available to me. I am no longer denying my past or feelings; the focus of my energy is shifting from 'swirling' outward to 'descending' inward. I am capable of focus, of purposeful behavior, and of acting on my own behalf. This comforts me. I am finally available to myself."

RENEE: "I do not have the energy to focus my thoughts, time, and energy on my ex-lover any more. This depleted me of the energy I need to take to care of myself. His life is none of my business. Whenever I begin to get caught up in my ex-lover's life, I will turn toward one of these life projects:

- The launching of a fitness program that includes daily walk-runs and yoga.

- The development of my career and the daily goals I have set for myself.

- Relating responsibly to my widening circle of friends."

HALLIE: "Historically, the swirls that I would get into are rescuing and managing other people's lives. As I was approaching the end of my college career, instead of centering in my own life, I took on my first husband as a 'cause.' I encouraged him to get a job, found him an apartment, and helped him apply to colleges. After the break-up of my marriage, I stopped swirling for a while. I got in a camper van with my dog and traveled around the country for two years. I had a spiritual center. I was at home with myself. But I didn't know how to bring that center with me when I reentered a relationship with a man. It didn't take long for me to again get caught up in a rescuing swirl.

"I was truly dizzy when I joined a support group. My life was out of balance. I was fearful for my alcoholic stepson's life. I couldn't sleep. I cried a lot. I kept trying to figure out some solution to hand him. After months of panic and craziness, it dawned on me that I was no longer participating in my own life. By swirling in my adult stepchildren's lives, I was jeopardizing my own health, sanity, friendships, and professional commitments. That's when I began the journey back home to myself."

Descending into the Richness: Composing a Vow to Reclaim Your Natural Capacities

I have two very special eight-year-old friends— Moizee Simone Stewart and Carson Fox Young. They are my teachers. They remind me of a time—in the very beginning of my life—when I was full of myself. As we play, talk, sing, and adventure together, snapshots of that earlier time pass through my mind's eye.

Moizee moves through each day with exuberant strength, remarkable energy, and contagious liveliness. Her days unfold according to a deep wisdom that resides within her. It faithfully orchestrates her movements from crawling to walking to running; her sounds from garbles to single words to sentences; and her knowing of the world through her sensual connection to it.

Carson's purpose is clear: to live fully in the abundance of her life. With courage, she explores her world. Her ordinary life is interesting enough. Every experience is filled with wonder and awe. It is enough to gaze at the redness of an apple, to watch the water flow over the rocks in a stream, to listen to the rain dance, and to count the peas on her plate. Ordinary life is her teacher, challenge, and delight.

Moizee says a big "Yes" to Life as it pulsates through her body. With excitement, she explores her body. She is unafraid of channeling strong feelings through her. She feels her joy, sadness, anger, and fear. She is pregnant with her own life. She is content to be alone. She touches the depths of her uniqueness. She loves her mind. She expresses her feelings. She likes herself when she looks in the mirror.

At the buried core of women's identity is a distinct and vital self first articulated in childhood, a root identity that gets cut off in the process of growing up female.
—EMILY HANCOCK,
THE GIRL WITHIN

Carson trusts her vision of the world and expresses it. With wonder and delight, she paints a picture, creates a dance, and makes up a song. To give expression to what she sees is as natural as her breathing. When challenged, she is not lost for words. She has a vocabulary to speak about her experience. She speaks from her heart. She voices her truth. She has no fear, no sense that to do it her way is wrong or dangerous.

Moizee is a warrior. It takes no effort for her to summon up her courage, to arouse her spirit. With her courage, she solves problems. She is capable of carrying out any task that confronts her. She has everything she needs within the grasp of her mind and her imagination. She accomplishes great things in her mind, in her room, and in the neighborhood. With her spirit, she changes what doesn't work for her. She says, "I don't like that person" when she doesn't, and "I like that person" when she does. She says, "No," when she doesn't want to be hugged. She takes care of herself.

As I celebrate the remarkable capacities of these two girl-children, I am aware of critical words from my childhood and adolescence, echoing across the decades to challenge their fullness, and my own. These deeply imprinted words recount what happened to the precious being I once was—we all once were in the very beginning of our lives. Over time, the inner voice that led us into wonder-filled explorations was replaced by critical voices. As a result, the girl-child's original vision is narrowed; she sees the world as everyone else sees it. She loses her ability to act spontaneously; she acts as expected. Her original trust in herself is shattered; she waits to be told how to live. Her original spunk is exiled; she learns that it is dangerous to venture outside the lines. Her original goodness is twisted and labeled unnatural, unfeminine, or "too intense" by the adults in her life. She will grow up asking, "What's wrong with me?" This question regularly punctuates our lives as we search far and wide for someone to give us an answer, for someone to offer us a magical insight, treatment, or cure. We have learned a criticism-based way of perceiving ourselves and relating to the world. As a result, our automatic tendency is to feel inadequate, that we're never quite good enough no matter what we do.

While in seminary, I read a parable that reminded me of the sad reversals of childhood. In an adapted form, it has followed me through the years, finding its way from one journal to the next:

> In the dark of the night thieves entered a store and did their work without detection. In the morning the store opened at the appointed time. It was obvious to the clerk that the store had been entered, and yet nothing seemed to have been taken. As the day progressed and customers brought merchandise to the counter, the storekeepers began to notice a curious phenomenon. The merchandise of least value wore the tags of greatest value. And the items of greatest value carried the tags of least value. By the end of the day the puzzle had been solved. The thieves had reversed the price tags.

Sadly, a conformity-based childhood reverses the price tags: the natural and essential self, a priceless treasure, is demeaned and set aside, and the artificial and constructed self grows in perceived value. Image is more valuable than essence; conformity more priceless than originality; and lies are celebrated as truth. Throughout childhood we were offered a monumental choice: to tell the truth and be who we were, risking abandonment and rejection, or to conform by developing an artificial self in order to win the approval of important adults and to survive childhood.

From my own experience as teacher and friend of children, as workshop facilitator and spirituality counselor, and from the experience of the women whose stories I have read and listened to in countless

Our healing task is not to become a new, improved, or changed person. Rather, it is to reclaim our natural and essential self in all its fullness.

—PLR

circles, I have pinpointed eight natural capacities that constitute our potential for health and fullness. They were introduced in chapter 2:

Capacity 1.   The Girl-Child Is Body-Centered.

Capacity 2.   The Girl-Child Expresses Her Needs.

Capacity 3.   The Girl-Child Is Sexually Autonomous.

Capacity 4.   The Girl-Child Expresses Her Feelings.

Capacity 5.   The Girl-Child Tells the Truth.

Capacity 6.   The Girl-Child Is Interested in Herself.

Capacity 7.   The Girl-Child Is Creative.

Capacity 8.   The Girl-Child Is Full of Herself.

In some of our homes, these capacities were encouraged to develop and to flourish. In conformity-based homes, however, the natural and essential self was criticized and expected to be discarded on our way to becoming an acceptable female.

The fourth and most intensive vow process, "Descending into the Richness," dismantles the question "What's wrong with me?" and will support you in reclaiming each of your natural capacities. It will challenge you to embrace your essential self by discarding the facades and personas of a lifetime and to celebrate originality and truth by shedding the conformity of many lifetimes. No longer content with self-improvement schemes or feminist platforms that merely require a rearrangement of your outer life, you will "descend into the richness" and experience the transformation of your inner world. This process will support your decision to grow in knowledge and love of yourself and to compose the essential/transformational vow introduced in chapter 2.

If you are a parent, use the "Descending into the Richness" process to review your attitudes toward your daughters and to evaluate the family environment you have created. Are their natural capacities supported to develop and flourish? What is valued in your home: image or essence, conformity or originality, lies or truth? The chapter will support you to celebrate the gifts and address the challenges of your parenting style.

LINDA: "I am descending into the richness of ME. I am releasing all the thoughts, feelings, and artistic images that had been held captive. I thirst for the experience of myself. I am in the process of rebirth. I am making my own acquaintance through a thousand small and large recognitions. Yeah!"

ANNETTE: "As I 'descended into the richness,' every obstacle to self-love showed itself and was cleared away. It was a body-felt, in-the-cells, in-touch-with-the-truth-of-myself experience. It restructured my entire inner world. I have an expanded sense of who I am. I'm more present to myself. I've set important boundaries. I speak up in the moment. I see myself as a creative being."

ERIN: "My solitude is comfortable. I embrace my aloneness. The life I have now will stay intact no matter what man is in my life at any given time. I will always keep spaces open for myself. A relationship, or many relationships, are but a small part of the whole of me. I choose the ways I want to fit men into my life schedule. No longer does my life revolve around them. I turn all my energy toward myself: my spirituality, my women friends, my job, and my children. My commitment to myself reminds me that I am the center of my universe from which all else flows."

CHRISTINE: "I have abstained from sexual relationships for four years. My life has improved on all levels. I have slowed down. I am learning to have a relationship with myself. My friendships are deeper. I completed my B.A. degree and have begun a Master's program. My relationship to money has improved. All in all, my life is manageable and full. At other times when I've been "unattached," I was either swirling over my previous relationship or looking for someone new. For brief periods I would take positive actions on my own behalf, but I always had one eye out for the next distraction. My vow keeps me grounded in my own best interest."

JAN: "I was groomed by my mother to snag a husband and then to do whatever was necessary to hold onto him. I passed this 'grooming' on to my daughters. My son was pampered by the women in the house. The girls were expected to pay attention to their weight and appearance in a way I never expected of him. I encouraged the girls' romantic lives by continually asking about boyfriends. I felt they should have a man in their lives. As I turn inward, my daughters are changing. I thought it was too late for them, that the damage to their sense of self was beyond healing. It turns out the 'self' is very resilient."

MARCY: "I vow to trust my body; it is strong and capable. I will take care of my body and make time for sensual pleasure. I will feel all my feelings and not minimize or block them. I will express them as I feel them. I will be willing to not only speak the truth but also to hear the truth. I will continue to find outlets for my voice and inner song. I will use my gift of song to please myself, others, and God. I will find time to be alone and allow myself to do as I please in that time, with no recriminations. I will seek to be still, so that I may hear God's voice and my own inner wisdom. I will continue to immerse myself in a community of women who are also on a spiritual journey and will leave myself open to the unknown possibilities and promise of a life lived with reclaimed capacities."

Moving through the Rest of the Book

Each of the remaining chapters is self-contained. Feel free to journey through the book as you are moved. Trust your own deep wisdom to lead you. If you are a mental health professional, clergyperson, or supportive friend, read through each chapter to increase your resource pool to offer to your clients, parishioners, friends, or colleagues. If you are preparing for your wedding or the birth of a child, begin with "Remembering Yourself" (chapter 4). If you are in a transitional season of life—ending or beginning a relationship, moving to a new location, graduating, grieving the loss of a loved one, or reframing your life after an unexpected diagnosis—begin with "Gathering the Gifts" (chapter 5). If you are estranged from your own life or swirling in someone else's, yet longing to return home, begin with "Discovering the Way Home" (chapter 6). If you are tired of asking the question, "What wrong with me?", are choosing abstinence from intimate relationships, beginning your healing journey, spiraling into and through a deeper layer of healing, or reviewing your parenting style, begin with "Descending into the Richness" (chapter 7).

FOUR

Remembering Yourself:
Composing a Vow to Prepare for Marriage
and/or the Birth of a Child

Imagine a woman who loves herself. A woman who gazes with
loving kindness upon her past and present, her body and its needs,
and her ideas and emotions. Whose capacity to love others deepens
as she extends loving kindness to herself.

Imagine a woman who accepts herself. A woman who has
descended into her own richly textured humanity, turning a merciful eye toward all that she discovers. Whose capacity to live nonjudgmentally toward others deepens as she is merciful toward
herself.

Imagine a woman who turns toward herself with interest and
attention. A woman who acknowledges her own feelings, thoughts,
and perceptions. Whose capacity to be available to others deepens
as she is available to herself.

Imagine a woman who fully participates in her own life. A woman who meets each challenge with creativity and takes action on her own behalf with clarity and strength. Whose capacity to participate in relationships deepens as she participates in her relationship to herself.

Imagine a woman who remains faithful to herself through all the seasons of life. A woman who preserves allegiance to herself even in the face of opposition. Whose capacity to sustain interest in others deepens as she is loyal to herself.

Imagine yourself as this woman ... as you enter into the "Remembering Yourself" process by setting aside fifteen minutes a day to "remember yourself." Begin each session with step 1—the "Home Is Always Waiting" meditation. Journal through steps 2 and 3 slowly and carefully, highlighting those words, phrases, and insights that resonate with your own experience. Your evolving vow of faithfulness will be the most precious gift you receive as you prepare for marriage and/or parenthood.

Step 1 Remembering Your Spirit: "Home Is Always Waiting" Meditation

Step 2 Remembering Yourself: Vow Composition

Step 3 Remembering Your Support: Creating a Ceremony

Step 1 Remembering Your Spirit:
"Home Is Always Waiting" Meditation

As you prepare for the future—your marriage or the coming of a child—it is essential that you stay present and in touch with life's organic resources: the groundedness of your breath, the wisdom of your woman-body, and the spirit resident within your life. Let us begin . . . present and at home. Home is always waiting. It is as near as a conscious breath, conscious contact with your body, and a descent into the creative resources of your inner life.

Remembering Your Breath: A Conscious Breath

Turn your attention inward by taking a few deep breaths. (Pause for two breaths.) Become conscious of the breath and its faithful rhythm, supporting you the length of your days. Savor the breath of life as it flows in and through and around you. (Pause for two breaths.)

On each inhalation, gather yourself from the far reaches of your life. Bring your energy and attention "home." On each exhalation, release the accumulation of your day. Allow sighs, sounds, and yawns to ride on the back of each exhalation to support your letting go, your settling into this moment. (Pause for two breaths.) Breathing in, gather. Breathing out, let go. (Pause for one breath.)

A few weeks back, I was sobbing in despair over my relationship. I tried all my concepts of God to calm me and nothing worked because my despair was so deep. Then I focused on my breathing. I breathed in and then I breathed out—over and over again. I said to myself: "If I can breath like all the other living things on the earth, then I can be certain that I have the Spirit of God in me. I am not alone." This was profound revelation and continues to support me in troubling moments.
—COLLEEN WEST

Affirm:
- ∞ The Breath, from which all life unfolds (Pause for one breath)
- ∞ The Breath, in which past, present, and future meet (Pause)
- ∞ Breath, I remember you (Pause).

Remembering Your Body:
Conscious Contact with Your Woman-Body

As you continue to breathe deeply, turn your attention toward your body. Make conscious contact with your body: move or stretch it, touch or massage it, or imagine the breath reaching into each part of your body. (Pause for two breaths.) Meet each body sensation with the breath and your own healing touch. (Pause for two breaths.)

If your attention moves away from home, away from your breath and body, away from this moment, notice the distraction without judgment, and then practice returning home. There will always be distractions. Our life practice is to return. Breathe again into this moment. Home is always waiting. (Pause for two breaths.)

Affirm:
- ∞ The Body, from which all life unfolds (Pause)
- ∞ The Body, in which past, present, and future meet (Pause)
- ∞ Body, I remember you (Pause).

Most of us live on a beggar's ration of air. The average person inhales one pint of air per breath, while our lungs can actually contain seven pints when fully expanded. This is one of the reasons that the range and depth of our experiences—especially sexual sensations—disappoint our longings. We simply do not breathe well enough to reach our full orgasmic potential in love.
—MARGO ANAND,
THE ART OF SEXUAL ECSTASY

Remembering Your Inner Life:
A Descent into the Rich Resources of Your Inner Life

The breath and body escort us as we continue our descent toward the rich resources of our inner lives. Imagine yourself as a leaf let go of by an autumn tree (Pause for one breath), a leaf slowly and gradually descending toward the ground (Pause for one breath), its descent cushioned by the breath of life (Pause for one breath), a leaf touching the ground in the forest deep within your being (Pause for one breath).

Make conscious contact with the ground of your being through prayer, an expression of openness, a movement, or in the quietness of the breath. (Pause for several breaths.)

Affirm:
- ∞ The ground, from which all life unfolds (Pause for one breath)
- ∞ The ground, in which past, present, and future meet (Pause for one breath)
- ∞ Ground of my being/Source of my life, I remember you (Pause for one breath).

Home is always waiting. It is as near as a conscious breath, conscious contact with your body, and a descent into the creative resources of your inner life. Ascend again into this present time and space, bringing with you the gifts of your descent.

Daughter of Woman, remember your spirit all the days of your life.

The myriad physical and emotional changes we experience throughout pregnancy give us unique opportunities to work intimately with many aspects of mindfulness—paying attention to our experience, being fully present, being aware of our expectations, cultivating acceptance, kindness, and compassion, particularly toward ourselves and our baby, and experiencing feelings of deep connectedness.
—MYLA AND JON KABAT-ZINN, *EVERYDAY BLESSINGS*

Step 2 Remembering Yourself:
Vow Composition

In your journal, record your reactions and responses to the following insights and questions. This will be the first draft of your vow. I have included portions of women's reflections to inspire you.

1. Your capacity to be available to others is in direct proportion to how substantially you are available to yourself. The vow-composition process invites you to turn toward yourself with interest and attention and to acknowledge your own feelings, thoughts, and perceptions. In this way, your capacity to be available to others will deepen. How will you:

   ∞ Turn toward yourself with interest and attention? (List one specific action.)

   ∞ Acknowledge your own feelings, thoughts, and perceptions? (List one specific action.)

Everything worth having costs something, and the price of true love is self-knowledge. It is for this reason that really becoming acquainted with yourself is a price well worth paying for the love that will really address your needs.
—DAPHNE ROSE KINGMA,
FINDING TRUE LOVE

Sample vows:

I will bathe at the end of each day. I will journal daily to record my thoughts, feelings, and perceptions.

I will type one of my journal-poems each day. I will call my best friend each evening to share the day's thoughts, feelings, and perceptions.

2. Your capacity to live nonjudgmentally is in direct proportion to how deeply you have accepted yourself. The vow-composition process invites you to descend into your own richly textured humanity in all its trouble and beauty, gift and challenge, awkwardness and grace, turning a merciful eye toward all that you discover. In this way, your capacity to live compassionately will deepen.

   ∾ Will you descend into your own richly textured humanity, turning a merciful eye toward all that you discover? (List one specific action.)

Sample vows:

I will acknowledge both my ineffective behaviors and my life-affirming ones each day in my journal. I will share both lists with my sponsor at the end of each week.

I will keep track of every time I judge someone in a day. I will then claim the judgment as my own and practice turning a merciful eye toward that area/issue/"blemish" in myself.

3. Your capacity to love others is in direct proportion to how deeply you love yourself. The vow-composition process invites you to gaze with loving kindness upon your spirit, body, heart, mind, creativity, and essential self. In this way, your capacity to love will deepen. Practice gazing with loving kindness upon all

*If we are depending on our partner
to make us whole,
we're in trouble.
Sooner or later, we shall feel betrayed.
Sooner or later, we shall hate the
    dependence,
Sooner or later, we may be the one
who does the betraying.
Wholeness is within.*
—MARION WOODMAN,
    COMING HOME TO MYSELF

aspects of yourself by reading through Therese's Baumberger's poem Fidelity. Use it as a starting place. Begin each line as she does and then personalize the following seven to nine lines with specific self-loving actions you will take.

I, _____, promise soul-fidelity,
To name my truths,
To speak and live them
With joy and conviction.
To nourish my spirit
With ritual, prayer, service.
With walks in sacred woods,
Communion with the Mother.

I, _____, promise body-fidelity,
To give myself only to those
Who treat me with passion,
Respect, and tenderness.
To feed myself good food,
To rest myself with sleep,
To dance and sing,
To celebrate my body

Human love consists in this:
That two solitudes border, greet,
and protect each other.
—Rainer Maria Rilke,
Letters to a Young Poet

With love and pleasure.

I, _____, promise heart-fidelity,
To know my feelings
And express them clearly,

To choose as companions
People who do the same.
To listen to my heart
When choosing my paths.
To call on friends
In painful times
To circle it with love.

I, _____, promise mind-fidelity,
To think the best of myself,
To still the critic's voice,
To feed it with learning,
Streams of new ideas
And time to ponder them.
Not to hide intelligence,
But to wear it like a crown.

I, _____, promise creative-fidelity,
To fill my home with beauty,
To frequent museums,
Theaters, opera houses,
Bookstores, and libraries.
To give myself the gift
Of writing prose and verse,
To play with new media,
To flow with grace.

A complete sharing between two people is an impossibility and whenever it seems to exist it is a narrowing, a mutual agreement which robs one or both of his fullest freedom and development. But once the realization is accepted that even between the closest human beings infinite distances continue to exist a wonderful living side by side can grow up. . . .
—RAINER MARIA RILKE,
LETTERS TO A YOUNG POET

I, _____, promise self-fidelity,
To respect my needs,
Maintain my boundaries.
To shower my being
With all that I can give.
To love myself entirely.
To marry soul, body,
Mind, heart, creativity.
To acknowledge that
I am a whole, complete.

4. Your capacity to participate well in relationships is in direct proportion to how fully you have participated in your life. The vow-composition process invites you to participate in your own life, meeting each challenge with creativity and taking action on your own behalf with clarity and strength. In this way, your capacity to participate meaningfully in your significant relationships will deepen. Will you participate in your own life:

   ∞ By meeting each challenge with creativity? (List one specific action.)

   ∞ By taking action on your own behalf with clarity and strength? (List one specific action.)

Sample vows:

I will create a "New Mothers' Circle" to meet weekly, and sign up for a bimonthly massage.

I have a full life today, including special friends, personal projects, and compelling interests. I will not elevate anyone to god status. I'm an active participant in work situations. I celebrate the talents and skills I bring to the workplace.

My job is depleting me. I refuse to use my precious life energy complaining about what isn't working. I will speak to my boss and arrange for a four-day work week. This will free up an extra day for my creative projects while the kids are in school.

My apartment is cluttered with the stuff of the past. Every time I walk into it, I cringe. I will spend this weekend sorting and cleaning. I will hire the neighbor kid to help once I've brought some order to the mess. When completed, I will invite my women's group over to bless the apartment's new life.

5. Your capacity to remain faithful to another is in direct proportion to the depth of your loyalty to yourself. The vow-composition process invites you to maintain loyalty to yourself through all the seasons of life, to preserve allegiance to yourself even in the face of opposition. In this way, your capacity to sustain interest in others and to remain faithful to them will deepen. Determine how you will maintain loyalty to yourself through all the seasons of life and preserve allegiance to yourself even in the face of opposition, by creating two columns in your journal. In column 1, list the present-day challenges/opposition to maintaining self-loyalty. In column 2, list the actions you will take to preserve allegiance to yourself, even in the face of opposition.

CHALLENGE	PRESERVING ALLEGIANCE
My fiancé is an extrovert. He expects me to keep up with his social pace.	I will educate him about my introverted needs. I will set clear limits.
My job requires me to ignore my ethical standards on a regular basis.	I will begin a new job search to find a company with compatible integrity.

6. Review your journal writings. Gather the words and phrases you have highlighted. Write a rough draft of your own vow. Allow the following vows to inspire you:

I, _____, will turn toward myself with interest and attention to acknowledge my own feelings, thoughts, and perceptions and to offer myself support through life's challenges and celebrations. I will cultivate my availability to myself by _____ and

_____. Without effort, my capacity to be available to others will deepen.

Any mother knows that her inflections, mood, and facial expressions can create calm or havoc. Children respond to our actions, even our secret feelings, in utero, and most obviously within our daily lives. Our words and deeds strike our children like lightning or reassure like a favorite doll.
—MARY HUGHES LEE, *MOTHER'S NATURE*

I will descend into my own richly textured humanity in all its trouble and beauty, gift and challenge, awkwardness and grace, turning a merciful eye toward all that I discover. I will cultivate compassion toward myself by _____. Without effort, my capacity to live compassionately will deepen.

I will gaze upon my past and present, my body and its needs, my ideas and emotions, my resources and capacities, my injury and exquisite potential with loving kindness. I will cultivate self-love by _____. Without effort, my capacity to love others will deepen.

I will participate in my own life. I will meet each challenge with creativity and take action on my own behalf with clarity and strength by _____ and _____. As I do, my capacity to participate meaningfully in significant relationships will deepen.

I will maintain loyalty to myself through all the seasons of life. I will preserve allegiance to myself even in the face of opposition by _____. As I do, my capacity to sustain interest in others and to remain faithful to them will deepen.

I, Patricia Lynn, vow faithfulness to myself within my significant relationship; I will be faithful to my need for solitude between times of closeness with my beloved: to integrate the experiences of our rich intimacy, to return home to myself, and to breathe into my being the healing, challenge, and comfort of our closeness. I will be faithful to my beloved friends and chosen family, incorporating regular times with them into my life. I will be faithful to my need for three days of complete surrender to my creative process: to follow its impulses, to nurture the business that sustains it, and to cultivate an audience to receive the fruit of my creative endeavors. I will be faithful to my need to sleep alone several nights a week and to wake up in my own bed on the days I choose for creative focus.

7. Write your final vow of faithfulness on a special page in your journal. Review your vow monthly or when faced with marital or parenting challenges. Update and renew your vow yearly.
Remember: Regular cultivation of your partnership with yourself is the best investment you can make in your marriage and family.

Step 3 Remembering Your Support: A Ceremony of Commitment

Many women choose to integrate the reading of their vows into already established rituals. Sarah chose to read her vow at the "Girls' Night Out" witnessed by her bridesmaids and a few close friends. Thea asked the folks planning her bridal shower to include a fifteen-minute "quiet time" to begin the evening during which she wanted to acknowledge her commitment to herself and receive words of support from those gathered. It then felt appropriate to turn toward the couple-oriented aspects of the evening. Susan asked folks to bring supportive words and symbols to her "Mother Shower," to escort her home when she wandered away from herself.

Some women choose to use the "vow of faithfulness" Ceremony of Commitment found in chapter 2. They personalize the script to reflect the setting of their choice and the metaphors in harmony with their spiritual beliefs. Invite your closest friend, minister, or rabbi to "officiate" at your ceremony. Some moms-to-be prefer the "Womb-Circle" ceremony. They enjoy the "birthing" movements and the active participation of their circle of supportive women.

THE WOMB-CIRCLE CEREMONY

Stand in a womb-circle with a group of trusted women: mythic figures who inspire you (bring pictures, statues, and writings), teachers and relatives who loved you in your early years (bring their photos and messages of support), and friends who support you today. Take a photo of this powerful circle of women. Display it to remind you of the support that is available to you daily.

The Gifts of the Nurturing Womb

THE CIRCLE:
"Daughter of woman, do you desire the gifts of the nurturing womb?"

THE WOMAN:
"Yes, I desire
to sit and rest for awhile;
to have my wounds caressed and my dreams held tenderly;
to cry on a shoulder; to accept the things I cannot change."

THE CIRCLE:
"Daughter of woman, receive the nurture, inspiration, love, and support of your womb-circle. Come let us hold you. We will caress your wounds. We will hold your dreams tenderly. We will gather your tears. Receive the gifts of the nurturing womb."
(The womb-circle rocks, supports, and enfolds her.)

"Daughter of woman, reach out whenever you need us.
Share with us your need for tender, nurturing support.
Allow us to be the feminine face of God to you."

The Gifts of the Pushy Womb

THE CIRCLE:

"Daughter of woman, do you desire the gifts of the pushy womb?"

THE WOMAN:

"Yes, I desire

an acknowledgment of my power;

the courage to change the things I can;

the support to say, 'No'; the courage to step into the unknown."

THE CIRCLE:

"Daughter of woman, receive the courage, stamina, willfulness, and power of your womb-circle. We acknowledge your power. We support your pushiness. We remind you of your courage to change the things you can. Say loud 'No's and clear 'Yes'es. Step into the unknown. Come let us thrust you into your life. Receive the gifts of the pushy womb."

(The womb-circle quickens its breath, contracts, readies to push her forth into the new adventure of parenting. The womb-circle's contractions become stronger and stronger. The circle breathes corporately. In the fullness of time, the circle pushes the mother-to-be into the new adventure of mothering/parenting.)

"Daughter of woman, reach out whenever you need us.

Share with us your need for courage, challenge, and strong support.

Allow us to be the feminine face of God to you.

Witnessing the Vow

THE CIRCLE:

"Daughter of woman, we are gathered to witness your vow of faithfulness to yourself."

THE WOMAN: (Reads her vow.)

THE CIRCLE:

"Inasmuch as you, _____, have grown in knowledge and love of yourself, and have vowed faithfulness to your own life and capacities, we now joyfully proclaim that it is right and good that you are woman. You are full of yourself!"

THE WOMAN:

"I value the women in my life. You are the feminine face of God to me. You remind me of the truth about myself when I forget. You escort me home when I wander away from myself. Supported by you, I will remain loyal to myself. Regardless."

FIVE

Gathering the Gifts:
Composing a Vow to Support Conscious
Transitions

Daughter of Woman, are you in that in-between life space, neither here nor there, stepping into the unknown as you begin a new life situation or leave a career, relationship, way of life, or self-understanding? Has the transition been thrust upon you—without your consent: Has the predictability of your life, relationship, or health shattered into a hundred pieces due to an unexpected diagnosis or the sudden loss of a job or loved one?

Is the transition chosen: Are you leaving a good job for an even better one, are you bringing closure to an effective therapeutic relationship, or moving beyond a no-longer working friendship or partnership? Is the transition part of the benevolent flow of your life: Are you graduating from high school, college, or graduate school, or celebrating a "milestone" birthday?

Daughter of Woman, participate in the challenges of your life, take responsibility for your decisions, feel your feelings, celebrate your own stunning capacities as a child of life. Firmly grounded in the present moment, embrace the lessons of the past and the possibilities of the future. Create a life strategy to address your challenge by tapping into your own resources of creativity and wisdom and by gathering pillows of support to accompany you through the challenging time. Firmly grounded in the present moment, take action on your own behalf with clarity and strength.

Imagine a woman who remains loyal to herself in tender times and turbulent times, in graceful moments and in awkward situations, in flowing times and in seasons of stagnation, in fullness and in emptiness, in fear and in courage, in trouble and in beauty. With all that she is and all she shall become from this day forward and forever. Imagine yourself as this woman . . . as you enter into the "Gathering the Gifts" process by setting aside at least fifteen minutes a day to "gather the gifts." Begin each session with step 1, the "Home Is Always Waiting" meditation. Journal through steps 2, 3, and 4 slowly and carefully, highlighting those words, phrases, and insights that resonate with your own experience. Your evolving vow of faithfulness will be your most precious companion as you walk through this transitional season of your life.

Those who don't love themselves as they are rarely love life either. Most people have come to prefer certain of life's experiences and deny and reject others, unaware of the value of the hidden things that may come wrapped in plain or even ugly paper. In avoiding all pain and seeking comfort at all cost, we may be left without intimacy or compassion; in rejecting change and risk we often cheat ourselves of the quest; in denying our suffering we may never know our strength or our greatness.
—Rachel Naomi Remen,
Kitchen Table Wisdom

Step 1 Gathering Your Spirit: "Home Is Always Waiting" Meditation

Step 2 Gathering Wisdom: Creative Reflection

Step 3 Gathering Yourself: Vow Composition

Step 4 Gathering Support: Creating a Ceremony or Life-Challenge Support Group

Step 1 Gathering Your Spirit:
"Home Is Always Waiting" Meditation

In times of transition, it is essential to stay present and in touch with life's organic resources: the groundedness of your breath, the wisdom of your woman-body, and the spirit resident within your life. Let us begin ... present and at home. Home is always waiting. It is as near as a conscious breath, conscious contact with your body, and a descent into the creative resources of your inner life.

Gathering the Gifts of Your Breath

Return home to your breath.

Turn your attention inward by taking a few deep breaths. (Pause for two breaths.) Become conscious of the breath and its faithful rhythm, supporting you the length of your days. Savor the breath of life as it flows in and through and around you. (Pause for two breaths.)

On each inhalation, gather yourself from the far reaches of your life. Bring your energy and attention "home." On each exhalation, release the accumulation of your day. Allow sighs, sounds, and yawns to ride on the back of each exhalation to support your letting go, your settling into this moment. (Pause for two breaths.) Breathing in, gather. Breathing out, let go. (Pause for one breath.)

Research and experience indicate that mind and body are not separate but part of a seamless, intricate network of intelligence. From a more intuitive perspective, your body can be considered a reservoir of cellular memory, wisdom, and guidance. If you attend it, it can richly reward your journey with understanding about your deepest being and about the ways in which you might find healing and wholeness.

—MARION WOODMAN,
COMING HOME TO MYSELF

Affirm:

- ∽ The Breath, from which all life unfolds (Pause for one breath)
- ∽ The Breath, in which past, present, and future meet (Pause for one breath)
- ∽ Breath, I gather your gifts (Pause for one breath).

Gathering the Gifts of Your Body

Return home to your body.

As you continue to breathe deeply, turn your attention toward your body. Make conscious contact with your body: move or stretch it, touch or massage it, or imagine the breath reaching into each part of your body. (Pause for two breaths.) Meet each body sensation with the breath and your own healing, acknowledging touch. (Pause for two breaths.)

If your attention moves away from home, away from your breath and body, away from this moment, notice the distraction without judgment, and then practice returning home. There will always be distractions. Our life practice is to return. Breathe again into this moment. Home is always waiting. (Pause for two breaths.)

"Watching over the breath" consists in letting the breath come and go as it wants, without forcing it or clutching at it. In due course its rhythm automatically slows down, and it flows in and out so smoothly. This is both a symbol of and a positive aid to letting one's whole life come and go without grasping.
—ALAN WATTS,
NATURE, MAN AND WOMAN

Affirm:

- ∽ The Body, from which all life unfolds (Pause for one breath)
- ∽ The Body, in which past, present, and future meet (Pause for one breath)
- ∽ Body, I gather your gifts (Pause for one breath).

Gathering the Gifts of Your Inner Life

Return home to your inner life.

Escorted by the breath and body, we continue our descent. Imagine your-self as a leaf let go of by an autumn tree (Pause for one breath), a leaf slowly and gradually descending toward the ground (Pause for one breath), its descent cushioned by the breath of life (Pause for one breath), a leaf touching the ground in the forest deep within your being. (Pause for one breath.)

Make conscious contact with the ground of your being through prayer, an expression of openness, a movement, or in the quietness of the breath. (Pause for several breaths.)

Affirm:

- ∽ The ground, from which all life unfolds (Pause for one breath)
- ∽ The ground, in which past, present, and future meet (Pause for one breath)
- ∽ Ground of my being/Source of my life, I gather your gifts (Pause for one breath).

Home is always waiting. It is as near as a conscious breath, conscious contact with your body, and a descent into the creative resources of your inner life. Ascend again into this time and space, bringing with you the gifts of your descent.

Daughter of Woman, gather the gifts of your spirit all the days of your life.

Step 2 Gathering Wisdom: Creative Reflection

Transitions invite us to reflect on where we've been and to gather wisdom for the journey ahead. The temptation is to create a new situation prematurely to "save" us from the awkwardness of fully participating in the transition. Firmly held in this present moment, I invite you to turn toward the job, person, program, or perspective you are leaving with an open heart and mind to appreciate its gifts and to learn from its challenges. In this way you will infuse the transition with clarity, consciousness, and gratitude. There are five parts to the "Gathering Wisdom" reflection.

1. Turning Toward

Gather photos, mementos, tangible objects and writings representing the situation you are leaving. Create a room-sized or table-sized display of the items you gather. Or write down your reflections in a special journal or notebook as suggested in the following examples.

2. The Challenges of Life

Journey through your display or written reflection, noticing what challenged you about the situation.

3. The Gifts of Life

Journey through your display or written reflection, noticing what delighted you about the situation.

The long work of turning their lives into a celebration is not easy....
—MARY OLIVER, "THE SUNFLOWERS"

4. Lightening the Load

Journey through your display or written reflection, noticing what actions you need to take to bring respectful closure to the past.

5. Gratitude

Journey through your display or written reflection, gathering the gifts of gratitude to take with you into the next season of life.

1. Turning Toward

To support your understanding of each aspect of the "Gathering Wisdom" reflection, we track the experiences of nine women:

∞ Heather was moving. She and her family had lived in the same area for ten years. She had seen her kids through the neighborhood elementary school and had developed a network of support that was comfortable. The job and commute were manageable. Life was familiar. She wanted to prepare for the move with great care and to say conscious good-byes to the folks her family had grown to love and respect. She didn't want to become so consumed with the details of the move that she had no time for the essential work of feeling the whole range of emotions that accompany a major move. She wanted to model a process of conscious closure for her children. For fifteen minutes a day, she and the children sorted through their drawers and closets, packing some things and displaying photos and mementos, representing their relationship to the community on their family altar.

Sometimes we may simply need to choose life. It is possible to become so attached to something or someone we have lost that we move forward blindly, looking over our shoulder to the past rather than before us to what lies ahead.... We are holding to something long gone and, hands full, are unable to take hold of our opportunities or what life is offering.
—RACHEL NAOMI REMEN,
KITCHEN TABLE WISDOM

∽ Susan was leaving her therapist of five years. She was ready to move on. She wanted to infuse this transition with consciousness because it represented a major milestone in her life. With her therapist's support, she had grown to trust herself: it was now possible to live her life and to navigate its challenges without the assistance of a trained professional. For fifteen minutes a day, she gathered: canceled checks, representing her investment in her own health and sanity; five journals, representing five years worth of inward exploration and self-discovery; and a calendar of life events, representing the major crises, challenges, and celebrations she had lived through consciously with the support of her therapist. She created an altar of gratitude in her art studio—a tangible representation of five years of hard work.

∽ Fourteen years ago Davita decided to leave nursing to became an accountant. Now, after fourteen years of working for the same company, she is ready to explore new opportunities. She could stay at the company forever. It is a good company with good benefits. She enjoys her coworkers and the cooperative attitude of the company. Yet her spirit was calling her to move beyond what was comfortable, to actively pursue other interests. She gave three months notice and for fifteen minutes a day, she gathered pay stubs, job awards, photos of office parties and events, and her accounting textbooks. She displayed these items on a large piece of fiberboard so it could be stored in a closet when she had guests in her small apartment.

We are daughters of life's generosity, constantly surrounded by the altruism of Mother Earth and the myriad blessings present in work and relationships. It is our birthright to joyously claim this bountiful inheritance.
—SUE PATTON THOELE,
THE WOMAN'S BOOK OF SOUL

꧁ Barbara was graduating from high school in three months. She was experiencing a mixture of sadness, relief, and excitement. She wanted to bring "conscious closure" to her high school years. She didn't want to carry baggage from one experience of life to another. She wanted to travel lightly and have access to all her life energy. She began gathering on Valentine's Day. For fifteen minutes each evening, she sorted through report cards, teachers' notes, yearbooks, photos, class schedules, event programs, notes from friends, and gifts from boyfriends. She displayed these items on a large table in her bedroom.

꧁ Jill was diagnosed with breast cancer. Knowing she would need all her emotional, physical, and spiritual resources to walk through the healing process, she wanted to "take stock" of the gifts of the past that might support her and to clear out anything that would interfere with her relationship to her body and accessing its healing capacities. For fifteen minutes a day, no matter what else was going on, Jan walked through each decade of her life using the "Gathering the Gifts" process. She divided the vacant bedroom into four quadrants, each representing a decade of her life. She sorted through boxes and boxes of memorabilia, placing letters, photos, mementos, report cards, résumés, and gifts in the appropriate quadrant.

꧁ Joan's divorce would be final in three months. She wanted to use the time until then to bring closure to her ten-year marriage with consciousness: to feel every feeling, to turn toward every memory, to deal with unfinished business. She wanted to let go of the past and step into the future at the final meeting at the lawyer's office. For fifteen minutes a day, sometimes longer when the "spirit" moved her, she gathered photos, gifts, and letters; memorabilia from trips, outings, and special events; and symbols and representations of the energetic nature of their connection. She created an altar of remembrance in her husband's old study, displaying all that she gathered.

∞ Helen was married at eighteen. She spent the next forty years supporting her husband's career. He died unexpectedly. After the funeral, she wanted to embark on a journey of self-discovery. She knew she must first turn toward the years shared with her husband, moving backward in time to see what glimpses of herself she might discover along the way. Decade by decade, she moved backward sorting through the stuff of a lifetime, dividing the floor into five quadrants, one for each decade they shared. She added a fifth quadrant to hold the glimpses of herself she received along the way. Friends came over to help her sort—one hour an evening for a month. After the sorting task was completed, she traveled through each decade using the "Gathering Wisdom" process. She invited a friend to tape her reflections about each decade.

∞ Jacqui was about to explore a new relationship. She had been unpartnered for five important years. She didn't want to leave this season of her life without acknowledging its gifts and challenges. She wanted to bring "conscious closure" to what had been. Rather than gathering tangible items to represent her singleness, she chose to write about each year. She divided a notebook into five sections and for fifteen minutes an evening she wrote about each year.

2. The Challenges of Life

Move forward through the years, represented by your display or written reflection. Pay special attention to the difficult years or experiences as you pass through them. If you are moved to, draw the hurtful experiences, write about the painful exchanges, or dance the awkward moments.

HEATHER'S FOCUS **Moving from neighborhood**
Painful Moments Disbanding of women's circle due to internal conflicts
Development built on forest land behind our house

SUSAN'S FOCUS **Five-year relationship with therapist**
Painful Moments Family's unwillingness to participate in therapeutic process

DAVITA'S FOCUS **Fourteen years with same company**
Painful Moments Periodic run-ins with angry manager
Overlooked for promotion

BARBARA'S FOCUS **Four years of high school**
Painful Moments Death of poetry teacher
Losing election

JILL'S FOCUS **Relationship to body during healthy years**
Painful Moments Husband's rejection and infidelity after weight gain

The most invisible creators I know of are those artists whose medium is life itself. The ones who express the inexpressible—without brush, hammer, clay, or guitar. They neither paint or sculpt—their medium is being. Whatever their presence touches has increased life. They see and don't have to draw. They are the artists of being alive.
—J. STONE

JOAN'S FOCUS **Marriage is ending**
    Painful Moments   The death of our first child
                            Discovering husband's affairs

HELEN'S FOCUS **Discovering herself after death of husband of forty years**
    Painful Moments   Husband's unwillingness to share financial knowledge

JACQUI'S FOCUS **Years unpartnered**
    Painful Moments   Social awkwardness at couple-oriented events

3. The Gifts of Life

Travel again through the years or experience, as represented by your display or written reflection. This time pay special attention to the delightful moments or years as you pass through them. If you are moved to, draw the joyful experiences, write about the comfortable exchanges, or dance the bright moments.

> HEATHER: "The Johnson children are the same age as my three children. This has been a blessing for all of us. The kids enjoy each other's company and have spent countless hours in cooperative adventures."

> SUSAN: "My therapist supported me through the death of my mother, breast surgery, and the departure of my son for college. I learned the necessary skills to navigate the shifts and changes of life."

> DAVITA: "I always enjoyed going to the office. The atmosphere was supportive. The communication was so clear that gossip was not necessary. Issues were taken care of directly."

BARBARA: "My math teacher was a gem. He offered the same opportunities to the girls as to the boys. There was no discrimination in his class."

JILL: "My body has been healthy for forty years. It supported me through the birth of five children."

JOAN: "Jack loved the children and spent quality time with them throughout childhood. His commitment to our family came first. As a result he refused lucrative promotions that would have severely limited his time with us."

HELEN: "I developed skills and capacities as a good mother and supportive wife that can now be used in service of my own life. Nothing has been wasted."

JACQUI: "During my five-year sabbatical from relationships, I developed significant friendships with women. No longer fillers between relationships with men, they are now the mainstay of my support."

4. Lightening the Load

Revisit your writings about the Challenges and Gifts of Life and determine what actions are necessary to bring respectful closure to the past. Do you need to make amends for your ineffective behaviors, express your appreciation, clear up an resentment, forgive yourself for ineffective behaviors, or celebrate your life-affirming ones?

HEATHER: "We will plan a 'Thank You!' party for the Johnson family. The kids will decide on the menu, design the invitations, and write a poem of appreciation for each of the children."

SUSAN: "I will invite my therapist to my art studio to view the artwork inspired by our work together and to travel with me through five years of gifts and challenges."

DAVITA: "I resent the free time my manager had while I was busy taking care of the department. I take responsibility for not taking care of myself. I didn't set clear limits about what I was and wasn't willing to do. I will make amends to myself: 'I will set clear limits about what I am willing and unwilling to do in every work relationship.' I will make amends to my manager for splattering him with my stuff: 'I have carried a resentment toward you since your promotion to manager. I have resented that you had so much free time while I was busy taking care of the department. I have come to understand that this resentment has nothing to do with you. I didn't take care of myself by setting clear limits about what I was and was not willing to do.'"

BARBARA: "Due to my discomfort with silence and my need to figure everything out, I forced my boyfriend to discuss every nuance of our relationship. My obsessive need to 'process'

I will not die an unlived life. I will not live in fear of falling or catching fire. I choose to inhabit my days, to allow my living to open me, to make me less afraid, more accessible, to loosen my heart until it becomes a wing, a torch, a promise. I choose to risk my significance; to live so that which came to me as seed goes to the next as blossom and that which came to me as blossom goes on as fruit.
—DAWNA MARKOVA

drove him nuts. I will make amends in a letter I may or may not send: 'Due to my discomfort with silence and my need to figure everything out, I forced you to discuss every nuance of our relationship. I realize now that my obsessive need to process irritated you. The ending of our relationship challenged me to befriend silence and to allow things to be. I wish you well across the distance.'"

JILL: "Jeff and I agreed to a monogamous relationship and to inform each other of significant attractions. We promised not to act on our attractions unless we reframed our original agreement. I resent him for breaking his commitment to monogamy. He acted on his attractions to women in airports, restaurants, and professional contexts. I will express my feelings in a letter I will burn: 'I have carried a resentment toward you since our break-up. I have resented that you broke our commitment to monogamy by acting on your attractions. We agreed to a monogamous relationship and to inform each other of significant attractions. We promised not to act on our attractions unless we reframed our original agreement. It is not OK with me that you disregarded and broke our agreements. I feel nauseous when I think of you. Your lies taste bitter in my memory. With this letter, I relieve my nausea by spitting out the bitter lies. As I burn it, my system is cleared out of any residual resentment.'"

JOAN: "Because I have never developed a relationship with my own sexuality, I expected my husband to fulfill all my of sexual needs. He ended up knowing my body better than I know it and eventually resented my sexual passivity. I will write him a note, acknowledging this ineffective behavior: 'Because I have never developed a relationship with my own sexuality, I expected you to fulfill all of my sexual needs. You ended up knowing my body better than I knew it and I now understand that you eventually resented my sexual passivity. The ending of our relationship challenged me to befriend my sexuality. I wish you well across the distance.'"

HELEN: "Throughout our marriage, I was willing to be my husband's ally and partner in the process of our growth and transformation. I sought out resources to support our highest intentions. I will celebrate my capacity to fully participate in relationships and to act with compassion for others and with self-respect for myself."

JACQUI: "I will host a party for my women friends to share the gifts of my five-year sabbatical from relationships. I will set up regular dates with them to be reminded of the truth about myself when I forget, to be escorted home to myself when I wander away, and to be challenged to remain loyal to myself. Regardless."

Continue to "lighten the load" by inviting a friend to listen to your list of resentments, your letters of amends, and your commitment to changed behavior. Conclude with a self-blessing: "I celebrate my capacity to acknowledge the past's influence on the present, to walk through the past, and to heal into the present. I am relieved of burdens that are no longer mine to carry. I turn toward my life in the present with renewed energy and attention."

5. The Blessing of Gratitude

Now that you have acknowledged the gift and the challenge of the situation you are leaving, it is time to embrace the totality of your experience with gratitude.

Bless the difficult years and hurtful experiences, the painful exchanges and awkward moments, by personalizing the following blessing:

Breathing in . . . In gratitude, I gather my years . . . my experiences . . . my memories.
  Breathing out . . . There is no blemish.
Breathing in . . . I bless the difficult years and hurtful experiences,
  Breathing out . . . The painful exchanges and awkward moments.
Breathing in . . . In gratitude, I gather my years . . . my experiences . . . my memories.
  Breathing out . . . There is no blemish.

Celebrate the delightful years and joyful experiences, the comfortable exchanges and bright moments by personalizing the following blessing:

Breathing in . . . In gratitude, I gather my years
  Breathing out . . . There is no blemish.
Breathing in . . . I celebrate the delightful years and joyful experiences.
  Breathing out . . . The comfortable exchanges and bright moments.
Breathing in . . . In gratitude, I gather the years.
  Breathing out . . . There is no blemish.

Gather all of the years and experiences, the delightful and the difficult, on an altar of remembrance. Display the mementos, read your writings, enter into a meditation of remembrance. When finished, sit quietly at the altar. Breathe into the fullness of your years, your experiences, your memories.

Breathing in . . . In gratitude, I gather the accumulation of my years, my experiences, my memories.
   Breathing out . . . There is no blemish.
Breathing in . . . The delightful and the difficult.
   Breathing out . . . I acknowledge them all with gratitude.

Step 3 Gathering Yourself: Vow Composition

Grounded in this moment where past and future meet, supported by the breath, it is time to turn toward the future. Imagine a woman whose vow is her north star, her guiding light, the faithful breath she returns to in the midst of the "creative chaos" of transition. A woman whose vow supports her to embrace her own life, valuing its lessons above the prescriptions of experts. Whose vow supports her to participate fully in the challenges of life, using them as an opportunity to sharpen her skills for conscious living and to deepen her partnership with herself.

Imagine yourself as this woman . . . as you compose a vow of faithfulness to yourself. There is no "right" way to compose a vow. Read through the

Embrace your ordinary life, whatever its wrappings, for in the embrace you will hear the whisper of Gratitude. Listen for her in the ordinary activities of your day, in the ordinary encounters with loved ones, and in the ordinary challenges that rise to greet you each morning. She speaks from the depths of you, in the voice of your ordinary life.
   —PLR

women's vows whose journeys we have been following. Highlight words and phrases that resonate with your own experience of transition.

- ∽ Susan had grown in knowledge and love of herself during her five years of therapy. She wrote a list of insights she had received about herself. Turning toward the future, she wove each insight into her vow. It begins with these words: "Having grown in knowledge and love of myself during five years of therapy, I now turn toward the future with confidence. I vow to remain faithful to the insights gained on my journey of self-discovery: I will celebrate my anger and strength. I will no longer look to men to express my assertiveness. I will celebrate my intensity of feeling and consciousness, energizing every task I set out to accomplish. I will celebrate my powerful perception, bringing clarity to my introverted adventures and to my extroverted inter- actions. . . ."

- ∽ Barbara brought "conscious closure" to her high school years. Turning toward the future, she wrote a vow of faithfulness to herself, beginning with these words: "I vow to travel lightly through my years. I will not to carry baggage from one experi- ence of life to another. I vow to hold in high esteem the inten- sity of my intelligence, vitality, strength, sensitivity, and sensuality. I refuse the self-critical mantra 'I am too intense.' I will celebrate my intensity as a gift of life and its expression in word, image, dance, and erotic interaction as the gift I offer back to life. . . ."

∾ Having cleared out anything that stood in the way of her body's healing capacities, Jill wrote, "I vow to incorporate self-celebration into my life as a healing resource. I will begin by celebrating my courage to heal into the present by rewriting the myths of my family history to more closely conform to my memories, by altering ineffective behaviors, by leaving disrespectful relationships, by learning to speak my truth, and by listening to and acting on my intuition. My courage will now support me to travel through this season of life with dignity and grace."

∾ Turning toward the next season of her life, Joan celebrated the life-affirming behaviors she was taking with her into the future. Her vow begins, "I vow to celebrate my spirit of adventure, supporting me to explore new paths, to try alternative ways of thinking and doing, and to challenge existing lifestyles and cultural patterns. I vow to celebrate my generosity, my delight in song and dance, my ability to listen deeply to my children, my sparkling intuition, my capacity to just 'be' in someone's presence, my love of my body when I see its reflection in the mirror, and my enjoyment of my spirit when I spend time alone."

∾ Turning toward the next season of her life, Helen decided to do the "Descending into the Richness" process outlined in chapter 7 to reclaim her natural capacities in service of her own life—this time. In the process, she remembered her teenage desire to become a pediatric nurse and vowed to fulfill it.

∾ Turning toward the exploration of a new relationship, Jacqui vowed, "I vow to bring into my new relationship: my ability to stay in the present moment, observing my feelings, thoughts, impulses, and behaviors, without judgment; my sense of humor; my strong desire to live a peaceful and compassionate life; my accountability for what I say and do; and my growing willingness to be vulnerable."

Now write your own vow. Follow your creative impulses, incorporating the words and phrases you highlighted throughout the chapter. Begin the vow with these words: "Grounded in this moment where past and future meet, supported by my breath, I now turn toward the future...." Review your vow monthly and renew it yearly. When faced with life challenges, review your personal vow. Regularly cultivate your partnership with yourself. It is the best investment you can make to guarantee graceful and conscious transitions.

Step 4 Gathering Support

Susan read her vow to her therapist during the get-together in her art studio. Barbara read her vow at a "Girls Only" graduation party. Jill read her vow to the oncologist and evaluated every healing option in light of its wisdom. Joan invited her closest women friends over the evening after her divorce was finalized. She read her vow, replaced her wedding ring with a ring of her own, and stepped into her own life and future. Helen discovered "herself" as she worked through the vow-composition process. She invited her adult children and their spouses to a picnic at which she read her vow and invited their support as she pursued her dream of being a pediatric nurse. It seemed appropriate to Jacqui to read her vow at her women's circle. She invited her friends to vow faithfulness to themselves as they witnessed her vow. The formal vow-composition process did not work for Heather and Davita. They concluded the "Gathering the Gifts" process with step 2.

Create your own ceremony or adapt the basic one found in chapter 2 to reflect the setting of their choice and the metaphors in harmony with your own spiritual beliefs. Invite your closest friend, minister, or rabbi to "officiate" at your ceremony.

SIX

Discovering the Way Home:
Composing a Vow to Reclaim Your
Natural Resources

Daughter of Woman, are you caught in the swirl of pleasing your boyfriend, of rescuing your adult children, of supporting your husband's career, of meeting the body-beautiful demands of the culture, of searching for the "perfect" self-improvement regimen, of fulfilling the expectations of a New Age philosophy or guru, of "saving" the planet? Are you whirling in a chaos not your own, losing touch with your breath, your body, and the grounding center within you?

Daughter of Woman, befriend the richness within you, reclaim your own natural resources. Redirect your energy away from the "swirling" patterns of old toward adventures of self-discovery. Recognize each impulse to step into the life of another as an indication of disconnection from yourself. Learn to pause, notice the disconnection without judgment, and then return home, making conscious contact with your breath, woman-body, and inner life.

Daughter of Woman, imagine a woman who has grown in knowledge and love of herself. A woman who has vowed faithfulness to her natural resources. Who remains loyal to herself in tender times and in turbulent times, in graceful moments and in awkward situations, in flowing times and in seasons of stagnation, in fullness and in emptiness, in fear and in courage, in trouble and in beauty. With that she is and all she shall become from this day forward and forever.

Imagine yourself as this woman ... as you enter into the "Discovering the Way Home" process by setting aside at least fifteen minutes a day to journey home. Begin each session with step 1, the "Home Is Always Waiting" meditation. Journal through steps 2 and 3 slowly and carefully, highlighting those words, phrases, and insights that resonate with your own experience.

Softly and tenderly. Wisdom is calling.
Calling for you and for me.
Come home. Come home.
All who are weary come home.
Softly and tenderly. Wisdom is calling.
Calling, O woman, come home.

—PLR

Step 1 Discovering the Way Home to Your Spirit: The "Home Is Always Waiting" Meditation

Step 2 Discovering the Way Home to Yourself: Vow Composition

Step 3 Discovering the Way Home to Support: Creating a Support Group

Step 1 Discovering the Way Home to Your Spirit: The "Home Is Always Waiting" Meditation

When you are caught up in the swirls of another, use the following meditation to remind you of the way home. Over time you will develop your own.

Discover the Way Home to Your Breath: A Reflection to Begin

As you return home to the deep breath you knew in the very beginning of life, your original body centeredness is reestablished. With each breath, you actively nourish the body, balance its systems, listen to the wisdom of its sensations, and participate fully in every body-centered activity. As you turn your attention inward, you are reversing the lifelong habit of focusing outside of yourself. As you gather yourself and what is nourishing on the inhalation, and then release the lives of others on the exhalation, you are participating in an organic rhythm that supports health on every level of your being. Conscious breathing will support you to pause in the midst of your busy life to pay attention to your bodily sensations. It is the voice of your organic needs for food, rest, orgasm, exercise, elimination, and touch. With each deep breath, you will become more skillful at discerning the intention and wisdom of each sensation. As you step into self-responsibility, you will meet the needs of your body with tenderness and grace.

To seek approval is to have no resting place, no sanctuary. Like all judgment, approval encourages a constant striving. It makes us uncertain of who we are and of our true value. This is as true of the approval we give ourselves as it is of the approval we offer others. Approval can't be trusted. It can be withdrawn at any time no matter what our track record has been. It is as nourishing of real growth as cotton candy. Yet many of us spend our lives pursuing it.
—RACHEL NAOMI REMEN, *KITCHEN TABLE WISDOM*

The Breath Grounds You

Stand. Turn your attention inward by taking a few deep breaths. Imagine that you are in an ancient forest. Imagine that you have roots like the trees that surround you. You are as grounded, as connected to Mother Earth as a tree is. You are held, supported, and nourished by Her.

Acknowledge the firm ground that holds you as you breathe deeply. The earth calls you to come home. Everything breathes in the forest. Savor the breath of life that flows in and through and around you. Inhale deeply, imagine the breath rising up from the rich earth beneath you, as you say in your heart, "I come home to my breath."

Release the breath into the cool and moist air around you, as you say in your heart, "My breath grounds me." Inhale again, I come home to my breath. Exhale, "My breath grounds me."

Notice the depth of your breath.

Close your eyes and place your hands on your upper chest. Inhale, expanding your chest with the breath. Exhale, slowly letting go of all of your attachments. Inhale again, expanding your breath into your upper chest and exhale.

Now place your hands on the sides of your rib cage. Inhale deeply, pushing the breath against your ribs like an accordion. Exhale. Again, inhale, deepening your capacity to hold the breath of life, and exhale.

About 21,600 times a day, you have the opportunity to catch the wave of your breath: mindfully inhaling . . . mindfully exhaling . . . with a gentle smile and full awareness.
—JOEL LEVEY AND MICHELLE LEVEY, *SIMPLE MEDITATION AND RELAXATION*

Place your hands on your abdomen. Inhale deeply, breathing into your hands, imagining the breath as a great wave filling your belly. This is a deep breath. And exhale as the wave retreats. Now try again. . . . Inhale, allowing your breath to fill your belly and exhale.

Bring your arms to your side and continue to breathe deeply into your abdomen. Visualize the breath as a wave. Inhale; the full swell moves into your abdomen, ribs, upper chest. Exhale; the wave retreats from the chest, the ribs, abdomen, leaving in its wake serenity. Your breath calls you home.

Breathe into your fullness.
Breathing in . . . I breathe deeply. Breathing out . . . I let go deeply.
    Breathing in . . . I receive of life's fullness. Breathing out . . . I live out of life's fullness.

Discover the Way Home to Your Body: A Reflection to Begin

Your body is an essential resource on the way home to yourself. If you are uncomfortable turning toward your body with tenderness and conscious, prolonged attention, your discomfort makes great sense. Most of us have developed chronic resentments toward our bodies because they are always falling short of perfection as defined by the culture, our families, a current lover, and ourselves. They are never quite good enough no matter what we do to them. Notice your discomfort without judgment, and then imagine it riding on the back of the breath to be released with each exhalation.

As you turn a merciful eye toward your body, you are committing the forbidden act, the essential political act, of loving your body as you once did in the very beginning of your life. With each loving

I have learned that to breathe slowly and deeply is not an invocation of death but an enhancement of Life. To breathe is to let go and to live fully. The breath is a newly found treasure that has offered me a surprising lightness. The breath gives me permission to live each small increment of time to its fullest truth. The breath supports me to set healthy limits that set me free. My spirit soars with my breath.
—ERIN LOUISE STEWART

gesture, you are honoring your body as the sacred temple of the spirit of life and embracing it as a community of support within you, a harmonious partnership of cells, tissues, organs, and systems. Enter into partnership with your body, improving conscious contact with it through meditation, and consulting it through each season of her life. Celebrate your body as an exquisite resource, a faithful ally, and a trustworthy companion. Pay attention to its sensations as faithful reminders of the way home. Home is always waiting.

Your Body Grounds You

As we move through this meditation, imagine the person or situation that is most likely to draw you away from your center. Imagine being pulled to the right and to the left.

Stand and imagine that you are in a moist forest. Take a few deep breaths. Imagine that you have roots like the trees that surround you. You are as grounded, as connected to Mother Earth as a tree is. You are held, supported and nourished by Her. Acknowledge the firm ground that holds you, as you breathe deeply. The Earth calls you home.

Inhale deeply, imagine the breath rising up from the rich earth beneath you, as you say in your heart, "I come home to my body." Release the breath into the cool and moist air around you, as you say in your heart, "My body grounds me." Inhale again, "I come home to my body." Exhale, "My body grounds me."

Our psychological being has been severed from our biological selves for so long that we are completely cut off from our true natures.
—ELINOR W. GADON,
THE ONCE AND FUTURE GODDESS

Acknowledge the gravitation pull, the attraction of our body toward the center of the Earth. Visualize light coming into you from the center of the Earth. The light fills you and holds you steady as you continue to breathe deeply. With each inhale, use a gathering motion to gather yourself from the far reaches of your life, to draw the remnants of your energy toward you. Gather all that has been scattered. Gather all the fragments that are swirling away from home. Draw yourself toward center.

With your eyes closed, firmly plant your feet about six inches apart.

- ∞ Start swaying slowly to the right, like a tree swaying in a gentle wind. You are supported as you sway by your pelvis, hips, and thighs. Return to center. Acknowledge your center, your roots, your groundedness. Home is always waiting.

- ∞ Sway to the left a few inches, like a tree swaying in a gentle wind. You are supported as you sway by your pelvis, hips, and thighs. Return to center. Acknowledge your center, your roots, your groundedness. Home is always waiting.

- ∞ Sway again to the right. Come to center. Acknowledge your center, your roots, your groundedness. Home is always waiting.

- ∞ Sway again to the left. You are supported. Return to center. You can always return home. You are grounded.

- ∞ Continue to breathe deeply and repeat the movement to the right and to the left, increasing the range of your sway to its limit. Experiment at your own pace with your limits in each direction. Always returning to acknowledge your center, your roots, your groundedness.

- ∞ Now repeat the movements in each direction, decreasing the range of your sway until you are standing in your center of balance. Breathe deeply. Acknowledge your

If you can listen to the wisdom
of your body,
love this flesh and bone,
dedicate yourself to its mystery,
you may one day
find yourself
smiling from your mirror.
—MARION WOODMAN,
COMING HOME TO MYSELF

center, your home. There are forces that draw us away from our center. We can always return home. Home is always waiting.

Discover the Way Home to Your Grounding Center: A Reflection to Begin

When you swirl outward, you are thrown off balance. When you spiral inward, you are drawn toward your center and you rest. The meditation invites you to turn inward. Instead of looking to a god or higher power outside of your life for salvation, journey home to yourself. Instead of ascending to enlightened states of being that involve the denial of the self, descend, look deep within to reclaim forgotten aspects of yourself. Reach beneath your obsession with flaws, beneath the accomplishments that mask your sense of unworthiness, beneath years of alienation from yourself, toward the goodness at your center. Discover that the good is deeply embedded within you. As you embrace your original goodness, your inner spaces will be cleared out and reclaimed as your own. You will find rest within your own life and accept all of yourself as worthy.

There will always be distractions. Our life practice is to return. Always returning home again. Home is always waiting. It is as near as a conscious breath, conscious contact with your woman-body, and a descent into the rich resources of your inner life.
—PLR

Your Inner Life Grounds You

A conscious life unfolds from the inside out. Your inner life has been called by many names and known by many images. Breathe into each name and image. Notice which one rings true for you.

Breathing in . . . Source of Life,
Breathing out . . . My life begins in you.

Breathing in . . . Ground of My Being,
   Breathing out . . . My life is rooted in you.
Breathing in . . . Deeper Wisdom,
   Breathing out . . . My life unfolds from you.
Breathing in . . . Truest Self,
   Breathing out . . . Integrity at the center of my being.
Breathing in . . . Heart Center,
   Breathing out . . . Compassion at the center of my being.
Breathing in . . . Womb Center,
   Breathing out . . . Creativity at the center of my being.
Breathing in . . . Inner Sanctuary,
   Breathing out . . . Stillness at the center of my being.
Breathing in . . . Sacred Clearing,
   Breathing out . . . Spaciousness at the center of my being.
Breathing in . . . Intuition,
   Breathing out . . . Knowing at the center of my being.

Breathe deeply and discover your inner life.

Breathing in . . . I have descended
   Breathing out . . . into the rich resources of my own inner life.
Breathing in . . . I have returned home
   Breathing out . . . to the grounding center within me.

Your Grounding Center

Where is the grounding center within you? Allow your healing imagination to lead you there. As you move through this meditation, images may come to you. Draw them in your journal or sketchpad. Or reflect on them in the quietness of your breath and healing imagination.

Breathe deeply and rediscover your grounding center. Imagine your grounding center as a clearing deep within the forest of your being. Descend into your sacred clearing and touch holy ground. Your life is rooted firmly in the ground of your being. Your life is not fragile. It will not fall apart. Here in the sacred clearing you will rediscover the rich resources of your inner life.

There is a stream of living water that flows in and through and around the sacred clearing. Sit or recline in the middle of the stream of power and wisdom; dive deeply into its flowing waters or sit quietly on its bank, noticing its faithful flow. Allow yourself to become one with its flow. Breathe into the flow of life. Move the flow through your body.

114

A true mystic believes that all have an inward life into which as unto a secret chamber one can retreat at will. In this inner chamber one finds a refuge from the ever-changing aspects of outward existence; from the multitude of cares and pleasures and agitations which belong to the life of the senses; from human judgments; from all change, chance, turmoil, and distraction. One finds there, first repose, then an awful guidance, a light which burns and purifies, a voice which subdues; one finds herself in the presence of her god.
—CAROLINE STEPHENS

The stream invites us to lay down the responsibilities you were not meant to carry: The life choices of a loved one. The moodiness of a friend. The addiction of a coworker. The struggle of an adolescent. The depression of a relative. The changing nature of life. It is immensely wise to lay down these burdens, to turn them over to a wisdom deeper than your own, to let them go into the stream of living water, to release them into the wise flow of life. As the stream reminds you of a situation, concern, person, or relationship you cannot change, let it go into the stream, naming it in the quietness of your heart or aloud into the space. Be relieved of responsibilities not yours to carry.

Now reach into the stream and receive what it is you need this day. Acknowledge your need in the quietness of your heart or aloud into the space. Do you need: A steadying serenity? A powerful guidance? A comforting voice? A faithful presence? Do you need: Illumination? Courage and wisdom? Perspective, refreshment, and healing? Reach into the stream and receive what you need. You have everything you need within the rich resources of your spiritual center.

For the final moments of this meditation, in the quietness of your healing imagination or in your journal-sketchpad, reflect on the images that surfaced for you during the meditation. Draw them. Dance them. Write them. Breathe into them. Return home to the rich resources of your grounding center.

Daughter of Woman, return home to your breath, your woman-body, and to the grounding center within you. Serenity awaits you there.

Step 2 Discovering the Way Home to Yourself: Vow Composition

When we are caught up in the swirls of others, they become a burden to us. Settled and grounded in the serenity and responsibility of our own lives, we become free to support others in ways that enhance them and do not dizzy or burden us. Over the years I have developed a set of three relationship skills to support women to befriend their own lives and to honor the lives of others across a respectful distance. Practice these skills daily until they become deeply embedded in your relationships.

Skill 1 Letting Go of Overresponsibility

Practice the threefold acknowledgment process using a past or current swirl.

Acknowledgment 1

I am not responsible for the swirling thoughts, feelings, behaviors and actions of _____. I become dizzy when I step into his/her swirls.

Acknowledgment 1 reminds us that we are limited and finite, that there are some things we cannot change no matter how hard we try, no matter how desperately we want to rescue, fix, or work things out, no matter how genuine our concern or profound our love. There are some responsibilities we were not meant to carry: The life choices of a loved one. The moodiness of a friend. The addiction of a coworker. The struggle of an adolescent. The depression of a relative. The changing nature of life. Acknowledgment 1 not only reminds us that we are not responsible, it reminds us of the organic consequences of stepping into the swirls of others. We become dizzy.

Personalize Acknowledgment 1 by naming the particular person and the nature of their swirls, and by outlining the particular ways you become dizzy :

I am not responsible for the swirling thoughts, feelings, behaviors, and actions of _____. I become dizzy when I step into his/her swirls: _____, _____, _____, and _____.

Acknowledgment 2

I have come to believe that there is a Deeper Wisdom at work in his/her life and in my own. The Deeper Wisdom restores me to the serenity of my own life and reminds me of the way home.

Acknowledgment 2 invites us to remember the god of our understanding. The use of the word "Deeper" acknowledges that a woman's journey is one of descent. Instead of looking to a god or higher power outside of our lives, we look deep within to reclaim forgotten aspects of ourselves. The use of "wisdom" acknowledges that in our descent we rediscover the original Wisdom that orchestrated our days and development in the very beginning of life. We have come to believe that Deeper Wisdom restores us to wholeness and to a loving relationship with ourselves and others.

Personalize Acknowledgment 2, naming the swirl and using the metaphors in harmony with your own spiritual beliefs:

I have come to believe that there is a Deeper Wisdom/God/Goddess at work in _____ _____'s life and in my own. Deeper Wisdom/God/Goddess restores me to the serenity of my own life and reminds me of the way home.

Acknowledgment 3

I turn _____ over to the Wisdom of his/her own process.
I will not violate _____'s intellectual, spiritual, emotional boundaries.
Across the distance, I choose to honor and respect _____'s sacred journey.

Acknowledgment 3 invites us to take responsibility for the ways we have trespassed the lives of others. When we get caught up in the swirls of another, we assume we know what is best for them. We trespass their thoughts, feelings, and behaviors. We are invited to lay down responsibilities we were not meant to carry, to "turn them over" to a wisdom deeper than our own, to let them go into the wise flow of life. We choose against arrogantly intruding into someone else's life process. It is impossible for us to know the Deeper Wisdom for another person's life. Acknowledgment 3 invites us to accept that even between the closest human beings infinite distances continue to exist. It invites us to love the distance by seeing the "other" whole and against a wide open sky!

Personalize Acknowledgment 3:

I turn _____ over to the Wisdom of his/her own process. I will not violate _____'s intellectual, spiritual, emotional boundaries. Across the distance, I choose to honor and respect _____'s sacred journey.

May these examples inspire you to let go:

- ∞ Acknowledgment 1: I am not responsible for the swirling thoughts, feelings, behaviors and actions of my alcoholic son. I become exhausted when I step into his swirls to try to rescue him. I neglect important work responsibilities because he consumes my thoughts.

- ∞ Acknowledgment 2: I have come to believe that there is a Deeper Wisdom at work in his life and in my own. He will find his own way in the fullness of time—not to be orchestrated by me. The Deeper Wisdom will restore me to the serenity of my own life and will remind me of the way home to myself and to the fulfillment of my own personal responsibilities.

- ∞ Acknowledgment 3: I turn my son over to the Wisdom of his own process. Across the distance, I choose to honor and respect his sacred journey. I will not violate his boundaries by opening his mail, listening to his phone conversations, or monitoring his money.

∞ Acknowledgment 1: I am not responsible for the swirling moodiness of my young adult daughter when she arrives home from a job that she hates. I become exhausted when I try to convince her of how much happier she'd be if she found a new job. I neglect my own need for a walk and forego a break from her children after a day at home with them.

∞ Acknowledgment 2: I have come to believe that there is a Deeper Wisdom at work in her life and in my own. She will change things when she is ready or when she is miserable enough. The Deeper Wisdom will restore me to the serenity of my own life and will remind me of the way home to myself and to the fulfillment of my own self-care responsibilities.

∞ Acknowledgment 3: I turn my daughter over to the Wisdom of her own process. I will not violate her boundaries. Across the distance, I choose to honor and respect her sacred journey.

Skill 2 Clear Communication Across a Respectful Distance

Most of us were not given encouragement to develop healthy boundaries in our family of origins. Returning home to ourselves reestablishes internal and external boundaries. From the serenity of our own lives, we acknowledge what works and what doesn't work; we decide whether the swirling behavior of another—as that behavior impacts us—is acceptable or unacceptable. If unacceptable, we determine, and then articulate, a clear boundary without arrogance or judgment. Practice with this formula until you develop your own: "When

you _____, I feel _____. I would appreciate it if
_____.

May these examples inspire your boundary setting:

- ◌ When you smoke in my house, I feel uncomfortable and my throat becomes irritated. I would appreciate it if you would not smoke in the house again.

- ◌ When you continue to work in your office after I arrive home from work without acknowledging my presence, I feel disrespected and angry. I would appreciate fifteen minutes of reconnection time with you.

Skill 3 Self-Responsibility: Acting on Your Own Behalf

As we let go of our futile attempts to change those things that cannot be changed, there is an abundance of energy available to turn toward those things we *can* change. Ours is always a twofold admission. Yes, we are limited and finite *and* we are powerful and gifted. There are many things we can change. Courage is available to step into full responsibility for yourself: to design your own life; to author your own relationships; to name your own gods; and to exert, initiate, and move on your own behalf in your relationships, in your workplace, and in the world.

As women come home to themselves, they do not have the time or energy to get caught up in the swirls of others. Their own lives demand their full energy. The lives of others become none of their business. Whenever they begin to obsess about someone else's life, they choose instead to focus on their own creative projects, life concerns, and personal challenges.

Think of three personal or professional projects that have been clamoring for your attention. Describe them, along with your vow to focus your time, energy, and attention in service of the project. Be specific in terms of: the time you will set aside for it, the place in which you will turn toward it, and the support you need in order to complete it. Practice with this formula until you develop your own:

I do not have the time or energy to get caught up in _____'s life. My own life demands my energy. _____'s life is none of my business. When ever I begin to assume inappropriate responsibility for the life of _____, I will reestablish conscious contact with my breath and body, and the grounding center within me. I will remember my vow of faithfulness to myself and turn toward one of my life-projects: _____, _____, or _____.

May these examples help to inspire your vow of faithfulness to yourself:

> RENEE: "I do not have the energy to focus my thoughts, time, and energy on my ex-lover any more. This depletes me of the energy I need to take to care of myself. His life is none of my business. Whenever I begin to get caught up in my ex-lover's life, I will reestablish conscious contact with my breath and body, and the grounding center within me. I will remember my vow of faithfulness to myself and turn toward one of these life projects:
>
> • The launching of a fitness program that includes daily walk-runs and yoga;
>
> • The development of my career and the daily goals I have set for myself;

- Relating responsibly to my widening circle of friends."

KAREN: "I will not be diverted from the projects in my life by making senseless comparisons between my life and those of my friends and associates. If others have something in their lives that I want and can reasonably attain, I will act to get it for myself, rather than feeling victimized. Whenever I am tempted to get caught up in the swirl of useless comparisons, I will reestablish conscious contact with my breath and body, and the grounding center within me. I will remember my vow of faithfulness to myself and turn toward one of these life projects:

- Increasing the number of social contacts in my life;
- Taking the risk to sign up for a ceramics class;
- Putting in regular work on my dissertation topic."

JANET: "I do not have the time or the energy to get caught up in the swirls of my past. My current life demands my energy. I do not need to resolve every unpleasant occurrence of my past before I can choose to live in the present. Whenever I begin to obsess about my past life, I will reestablish conscious contact with my breath and body, and the grounding center within me. I will remember my vow of faithfulness to myself and turn toward one of these life projects:

- Centering on my breath;
- Playing in my garden;

- Taking the time to read;
- Spending time with creative activities and conscious people."

Step 3 Discovering the Way Home to Support: Creating a Support Group

Many women do not create a formal ceremony to conclude the "Returning Home" process. Instead, they gather friends together and create a project support group. Each session begins with the "Home Is Always Waiting" meditation and the reading of each woman's vow of faithfulness. The meditation reestablishes conscious contact with the grounding resources of breath, body, and inner life, and the regular reading of vows supports women to turn toward their life projects regularly. Through project introductions, ongoing project reports, and a culminating project celebration, each woman stays grounded in her own life and committed to her own projects—therefore she does not have the time, energy, or attention to swirl in the lives of others.

At the first session, after the meditation and vow reading, each woman shares her personalization of the relationship skill process. This will provide the context for regular and effective group support. If you interested in creating a project support group, familiarize yourself with the following overview, making alterations to fit the particularities of your own group:

Project Support Group

   ∾ Group Size: Six Women

   ∾ Session Length: Two Hours

Session Format:

- First Hour: "Home Is Always Waiting" Meditation and Reading of Vows

- Second Hour:

Week 1	Relationship Skill Review
Weeks 2-3	Project Introductions
Weeks 4-5	Project Reports
Weeks 6-7	Project Celebrations

Session Description

Project Introduction: Twenty Minutes per Woman

- Sit quietly for a moment and imagine the completion of your project. What does it look like? Describe its color, shape, taste, smell. Does it move? How many pages, sessions, hours will it be? Who will read it, attend it, sign up for it, wear it, listen to it?

- Breathe into your belly and expand your capacity to conceive of your completed project.

- Gather samples, outlines, pictures, music, poems, and any other "show and tell" items to introduce your project to the group.

- Determine whether you want feedback from group members. If you do, factor a feedback session into your twenty minutes.

Project Reports: Twenty Minutes per Woman

∞ Share with group the fruit of the previous week's actions. For example:

> One page a day of journal writing;
> Three questions answered about business opportunities;
> Five follow-up phone calls to potential clients.

∞ Determine whether you want feedback from group members. If you do, factor a feedback session into your twenty minutes.

Project Celebration: Twenty Minutes per Woman

∞ Create a ritual of self-celebration, honoring each step you took in your unfolding creative process. Share with the group your ongoing vision of the project.

∞ Determine whether you want feedback from group members. If you do, factor a feedback session into your twenty minutes.

∞ Love the sounds, movements, ideas, images, and words that emerge from you. Love them passionately. If the creative impulse includes sharing them, be full of yourself as you offer them without hesitation to appropriate audiences. Love the fruit of your creative womb.

If you prefer to create a ceremony rather than a support group, personalize the "vow of faithfulness" Ceremony of Commitment found at the end of chapter 3.

SEVEN

Descending into the Richness: Composing a Vow to Reclaim Your Natural Capacities

Daughter of Woman, your healing task is not to become a new, improved, or changed person. Rather, it is to reclaim your natural and essential self in all its fullness. In the very beginning, you remembered yourself. You came into the world with feelings of omnipotence, not inferiority. You loved your body, expressed its needs, and followed its impulses. You recognized and expressed your feelings. You told the truth. You were interested in yourself and enjoyed private time. You were involved with yourself and your own pursuits. You expected acknowledgment for your creativity and accomplishments. Reclaim your eight natural capacities. Support them to develop and to flourish. They are:

1. The capacity to fully dwell in your body and its natural vitality.
2. The capacity to recognize and express your body's organic needs.
3. The capacity to meet your own sexual needs.
4. The capacity to recognize and express your feelings.
5. The capacity to trust your own perceptions and to tell the truth.
6. The capacity to sustain interest and involvement in your own pursuits.

7. The capacity to create from your own unique vision of the world.

8. The capacity to celebrate yourself, welcoming recognition and acknowledgment.

Imagine a woman who has grown in knowledge and love of herself. A woman who has vowed faithfulness to her natural capacities. Who remains loyal to herself in tender times and turbulent times, in graceful moments and in awkward situations, in flowing times and in seasons of stagnation, in fullness and in emptiness, in fear and in courage, in trouble and in beauty. With all that she is and all she shall become from this day forward and forever. Imagine yourself as this woman . . . as you enter into the ten-step "Descending into the Richness" process by setting aside thirty minutes a day to "descend." Spend at least two half-hour sessions journaling through steps 1 through 8 slowly and carefully, highlighting those words, phrases, and insights that resonate with your own experience. Steps 9 and 10 culminate the "Descending into the Richness" vow-composition process.

Step 1   Reclaim Your Capacity to Love Your Body
Step 2   Reclaim Your Capacity to Befriend Your Body's Needs
Step 3   Reclaim Your Sexual Autonomy
Step 4   Reclaim Your Expression of the Full Range of Emotion
Step 5   Reclaim Your Capacity to Speak Your Truth
Step 6   Reclaim Your Solitude
Step 7   Reclaim Your Original Creativity
Step 8   Reclaim Your Capacity to Be Full of Yourself!
Step 9   Compose the Final Draft of Your Vow
Step 10 Design a Ceremony of Commitment

Nursery tales say that apples are golden to refresh the forgotten moment when we first found out that they were red or green. Fairy tales make rivers run with wine to make us remember for one wild moment that they run with water.
—G. K. CHESTERTON

Step 1 Reclaim Your Capacity to Love Your Body

Remember Your Birthright

In the very beginning, the girl-child's body is full of energy, movement, and sound. She lives a body-centered existence and is naturally exuberant. She releases her big bundle of body energy through movements and sounds. She runs and jumps, climbs and explores, throws and hits. She cries, moans, and screams. She shouts, sings, and hums. Even her occasional "tantrum" at the end of a long day serves to release her pent-up energy before sleep. Every body movement and expression teaches her where she ends and others begin—early on she doesn't know the difference between hitting a chair and hitting her brother, between climbing on the couch and climbing on Grandma's precious antique chair. Her senses are attuned to the world around her. She is naturally curious about the sight, sound, taste, feel, and smell of things. Most of what she will learn in the first five years of life, she will learn through her body and its capacities. It is her teacher, her healer, and her challenge. No separation exists between her mind and body. They are one within her. The exuberance of the universe pulsates through her.

Some women have vivid memories of their childhoods. If that is true for you, remember your original body-centeredness: the times when you ran free like the wind or jumped high like a horse; the

A child's world is fresh and new and beautiful, full of wonder and excitement. It is our misfortune that for most of us that clear-eyed vision, that true instinct for what is beautiful and awe-inspiring, is dimmed and even lost before we reach adulthood. If I had influence with the good fairy who is supposed to preside over the christening of all children, I should ask that her gift to each child be a sense of wonder so indestructible that it would last throughout life, as an unfailing antidote against boredom and the disenchantments of later years, the sterile preoccupation with things that are artificial, the alienation from the sources of our strength.

—RACHEL CARSON,
A SENSE OF WONDER

times when you climbed a tree or fearlessly crossed a creek; the times when you wrestled a friend to the ground and then tumbled down a hill; or a time when your voice rose up within you and was heard by the whole wide world.

Others have no memories of the girl-child they once were. They ask, "Was there ever a time when I was in love with myself?" If you do not remember your childhood, remember the body-centeredness of your preadolescent daughter, granddaughter, or niece: a time when she followed her own impulse to dance up the aisles of the supermarket without embarrassment, or when she needed no instruction to climb the big oak tree in your backyard and refused to come down for lunch. Allow your daughter, granddaughter, or niece to awaken memories of a time when you loved your body.

Choose whichever of the following three activities moves you: Write your parents a note of appreciation for nurturing your body-centeredness. Write your daughters, granddaughters, or nieces a note celebrating their body-centeredness. Write yourself a note of appreciation for the ways you nurture your own your body-centeredness.

Childhood's Hurtful Words and Experiences

Eventually our exuberance and body-centeredness were criticized as unlady-like (not feminine enough) or tomboyish (too masculine) by our families. We were offered fewer opportunities than our brothers to develop our physical capacities and to stretch our bodies to their physical limits. Our brothers were taught to throw a ball. They were encouraged to play baseball. A girl's place was in the home, not on the field, we were told. We were expected to wear shoes and clothes that made it impossible for us to keep up with the boys. We were expected to limit the space we took up with our voices. A certain tone of voice was encouraged: wimpish and passive sounds that reflected our restraint. We were expected to limit the space we took up with our bodies: "ladies" sat still with their legs together or crossed. We were required to conform to these childhood commandments at the expense of our healthy body-centeredness.

Some of us conformed and became quintessential females to win the approval of our parents and to survive childhood. Sufficiently restrained, our natural body energy was directed away from body activity toward body grooming, away from spontaneity toward control. Groomed to be "ornamental," we spent inordinate amounts of time and resources twisting our bodies into the acceptable shapes of the culture. Some of us rebelled and refused to twist our bodies out of shape. We identified with the boys and sought to transcend the "weakness" of being female. We assumed an androgynous demeanor and attitude that meant we were unacceptable to the "ornamental" girls and that we never quite fit in among the boys either.

Whatever our choice, we became convinced that something was wrong with our bodies and their natural impulses toward activity and exuberance. Those of us who chose ornamentalism denied these impulses as "unfeminine." Those of us who chose a male-defined androgyny embraced them as "boyish." Either way, the girl-child's original goodness was twisted out of shape and labeled unacceptable by her family ... and eventually, by herself.

What words twisted your natural body-centeredness out of shape and encouraged restraint? Note the words in your journal. Choose whichever activity moves you: Write a note to your parents, expressing anger, frustration, or disappointment that they did not support your natural exuberance and body-centeredness to

Who cannot love herself cannot love anybody. Who is ashamed of her body is ashamed of life. Who finds dirt or filth in her body is lost. Who cannot respect the gifts of life given even before birth can never respect anything fully.
—ANNE CAMERON,
DAUGHTERS OF COPPER WOMAN

develop and flourish. Write a note to daughters, granddaughters, or nieces, acknowledging the ways you did not support their natural exuberance and body-centeredness to develop and flourish.

Healing Words and Experiences

One of the most effective ways to reclaim our birthright is to imagine a childhood that supported our natural body exuberance and love. I call these imaginings "Healthy Family Fantasies." Participate in the following fantasy through play, movement, touch, or in the quietness of your healing imagination. Trust your own impulse to sit quietly or to enact the fantasy. Enter into a childhood hoped for. . . .

Every Sunday night when everyone else is out of the house and you and your mother are home alone, you read together from *The Book of Woman*, a special book kept in a special place, brought out in special moments sometimes by your mother, sometimes by your father. A sacred book that tells the story of woman. Your mother begins, "You are enough, my dear daughter. You are blessed. Hold nothing in. Allow your body to take its shape. Love the shape of your body." And then you read to your mother, "You are enough, my dear mother. You are blessed. Hold nothing in. Allow your body to take its shape. Love the shape of your body." And beginning at the top of your heads, you and your mother begin your weekly dance in celebration of your bodies in front of a big mirror. Sometimes you giggle together all the way through the ritual. Sometimes you cry.

When we allow our true spirit to manifest itself, we are acting on all that we know lies within us. We cannot allow gender stereotypes to prevent us from becoming who we can be.
—MARILYN J. MASON,
MAKING OUR LIVES OUR OWN

Let us acknowledge our round heads.

>We nod them to say, "Yes." We shake them to say, "No."

>Yes. No. Yes. No. Yes. No.

>We massage our round heads so that our thoughts will take a nap for a while.

Let us love our hair. We touch it. Stroke it. Twirl it.

>We bless its curls, its straightness, its color, its texture.

>I comb your hair. You comb mine.

Let us love our eyes. We bless their color.

>Mine are _____. And yours are _____.

>We open and close our eyes.

>We honor our unique view of the world. I see you. You see me.

Let us love our ears. We trace their shape and size. We massage them.

>We love our unique reception of the world.

>I hear you. You hear me.

Let us love our noses. We bless their shape and size.

>We breathe in and out slowly.

>We honor the Breath of Life as it passes through us.

Let us love our mouths and lips. We trace the shape of our lips.

>We love the sounds of our mouth. We make sounds.

>Loud sounds. Quiet sounds. Funny sounds.

Healthy intimacy, trust, and self-empowerment all begin with touch for a girl child, because empowerment lies in following the body, not in imposing controls from outside. Touch also contributes to her sense of body affirmation, perception, and definition. A girl who has been touched in a loving and respectful will instinctively reject any intrusion on her body.

—Virginia Beane Rutter,
Celebrating Girls

Let us love our necks. We hold them up high pretending to be giraffes.

We roll our heads around on top of our neck.

We massage our necks to thank them for carrying our heads around all the time.

Let us love our shoulders. We raise them to our ears.

And then let them fall again. Up and down. Up and down.

I massage your shoulders. You massage mine.

Let us love our arms. We raise them up in front of us and shake them.

We bend them at the elbows. We bend them at the wrist.

We clap our hands together. We are applauding ourselves!

I kiss your hands. You kiss mine.

Let us love our breasts.

Firm, sagging, full, flat, beautiful as they are.

We trace the shape of our breasts.

Let us love our stomachs. We fill them with the breath.

We honor our round bellies, growing like a balloon.

We release the breath. We honor our flattening bellies.

I peek in your belly button. You peek in mine.

Let us love our genitals.

We trace our pubic triangle as it is now or as it will be in a few years.

We name the parts of our woman-bodies as we look at them in the mirror:

Pubic Mound. Hood. Inner Lips. Outer Lips. Clitoris.

Opening to Urethra. Opening to Vagina. Anus.

Let us love our bottoms—our gluteus maximus.

The biggest muscle in the whole body!

We trace the shape of our bottom.

We are grateful it's a comfortable cushion to sit on.

Let us love our legs. The top of the leg is the thigh.

We feel our strong thighs. We bend our legs at the knee.

The bottom of the leg is the calf.

I massage your calf. You massage mine.

Let us love our feet. We bend them at the ankle.

We spread our toes out wide. We bend our toes backward and forward.

We count each toe. This little piggy went to market. This little piggy stayed home.

We have dancing feet.

You and your mother put on your favorite dance music and finish your ritual by moving every part of your body in a joyful dance in celebration of your lively and strong girl- and woman-bodies!

Pause to remember a scene from childhood involving your natural body-centeredness. If your natural body-centeredness was supported in the scene, write the scene as you remember it. If your natural body-centeredness was not supported in the scene you remember, rewrite it. Enter the scene with your healing imagination: replace all critical words and persons with supportive ones. If the "Healthy Family Fantasy" touched or inspired you, read it again and again. Using it as your inspiration, review your schedule and list possible dates and times to experience a weekly body meditation with your daughter . . . with yourself.

Descent and Rediscovery

Imagine yourself as a leaf let go of by an autumn tree . . . a leaf slowly and gradually descending toward the ground . . . its descent cushioned by the breath of life . . . a leaf touching the ground in the forest deep within your being. You rise from the ground, thanking the leaf for transporting you so gently.

Everything breathes in the forest. Savor the breath of life flowing in and around you. Inhale deeply as the breath rises from the rich earth beneath you. Release the breath into the cool and moist air around you. Your attention moves upward and you notice the trees reaching arm in arm for the sky.

You become a tree. Your feet grow roots extending deep into the ground. Your arms become branches stretching high into the sky. You sway with the breeze. The birds of the forest dance with you as they leap from branch to branch. You see many things from your new height.

A nearby stream calls to you, "Come and play." In a moment, you are at the stream, splashing in its bouncing waters. As you are drying off in the warm sunlight pouring through the forest canopy, a path opens up before you and invites you to follow it to a special place. You accept the invitation and follow the path. The path leads you deep within the forest to the edge of a clearing . . . a magical open space surrounded by a ring of ancient redwoods, forming the outer circle, and by a sparkling stream, forming the inner circle. You cross the stream. You enter the clearing.

A woman approaches you: "The Mother of All Living is waiting. She has a gift for you. Come let us meet her in the center of the clearing." You see the Mother at a distance. You approach her with your arms at your sides. You feel no shame in her presence. Her eyes meet yours and in her gaze, you are recognized . . . shaken . . . and relieved. She embraces you and you become as you once were . . . fully present and in love with yourself. She hands you a beautifully wrapped gift. As you open it, she speaks, "Daughter of Woman, dance the sadness of a lifetime for what could never be. And when your sadness is quieted, dance with her partner, gladness. For as deep a cavern as sorrow has carved within you that shall be your capacity for joy. Dance your gladness for what is now and will be forevermore.

"Daughter of Woman, receive again your birthright. Run free like the wind. Jump high like a horse. Climb a tree. Cross a creek. Wrestle a friend to the ground. Tumble down a hill. Let your voice bellow and be heard by the whole wide world. Dance to the music of your own life in love with your body. It is your teacher, your healer, and your challenge. It is your faithful companion for the length of your days. Your body is good. It is very good. Be full of yourself."

Vow Faithfulness to Your Body

Imagine a woman in love with her own body. A woman who believes her body is enough, just as it is. Who celebrates her body and its rhythms and cycles as an exquisite resource. Imagine a woman who honors the body of the Goddess in her changing body. Imagine yourself as this woman as you vow faithfulness to your body.

Use the following activities to inspire, provoke, and give shape to your vow:

1. List the ways you nurture your relationship to your body in your journal. If you are a parent, list the ways you nurture your daughter's relationship to her body.

2. Create two columns in your journal. In column 1 list the present-day challenges or opposition to maintaining your relationship to your body. In column 2, list the ways you will preserve allegiance to your body against each challenge or opposition.

3. The Ceremony of Commitment includes the following questions. In your journal note the memories, feelings, and sensations that are triggered as you read each question and as you imagine answering, "I Will."

> Will you love your body all the days of your life?
>
> Will you touch it with tenderness and support it with strength?
>
> Will you honor its rhythms and cycles as an exquisite resource?
>
> Will you honor the body of the goddess in your changing body?

4. Allow women's vows to inspire your own. Highlight the phrases that resonate with your experience.

There have always been women who remember the old ways. Women who refuse to twist their female bodies out of shape to fit into definitions, to transcend limitations. Women who love their bodies. Regardless.

—PLR

I vow to look upon my body with a merciful eye and to trust its strength and capacity.

I vow to honor and acknowledge my body as a vital and sacred resource through regular exercise.

I will find a physical activity that I truly enjoy to support the well-being of my body, mind, and spirit.

I vow to use my body to explore the world and experience the limitlessness of my horizon.

I will end each day with a lavender bath.

5. Take a deep breath. Gather phrases from the exercises mentioned, sprinkle in some new ones, and compose a one- to three-sentence vow of faithfulness to your body.

Step 2 Reclaim Your Capacity to Befriend Your Body's Needs

Imagine a woman who trusts and respects herself. A woman who listens to her body's needs. Who meets them with tenderness and grace. Imagine yourself as this woman as you vow faithfulness to your body's needs.

Remember Your Birthright

In the very beginning, the girl-child is one big bundle of needs, and she expresses them very clearly. When she is hungry, she lets everyone know. When a food upsets her system, her body offers immediate feedback in the form of a rash or stomachache, or in the clear dislike of that food in the future. When she's tired, she falls asleep wherever she may be—in someone's arms or on the department store floor. And when she hasn't gotten enough sleep, her whole being is out of balance until her life energy has been restored. When she is cold, she wraps up. When she is hot, she strips wherever she may be. When her body needs to expel gas, she farts or burps without hesitation. When her body is ready to eliminate the day's waste, she demands that a bathroom be found however inconvenient it may be. When she wants to be hugged or held, she crawls onto someone's lap.

She loves the feel of her blanket touching her face; the feel of the mud and sand touching her feet; and the feel of the water touching her whole body as she swims or takes a bath. Touch is essential to her healthy development. In her mother's womb, it soothed and comforted her. And on her trip down the birth canal, she was pushed, pulled, and hugged her into life by the laboring action of her mother's body. The organic needs and impulses of the universe pulsate through her.

Pause to remember your childhood awareness of your own organic needs and impulses: a time when you were aware of your need to sleep, to eat, or to bundle up, and expressed it however inconvenient it may have been to the adults; a time when you were certain a food was not what your body needed; a time when you reveled in the feel of the mud, sand, or water touching your body.

If you do not remember the very beginning, recall your preadolescent daughter, granddaughter, or niece's awareness and expression of her organic needs: a time in her life when she burped or farted without hesitation; a time when she refused to take another step in the department store and fell asleep outside the fitting room. Allow your daughter, granddaughter, or niece to awaken memories of a time when you were in touch with your body's needs.

Choose whichever of the following three activities moves you: Write your parents a note of appreciation for nurturing your awareness of your body's needs and your growing capacity to express and meet them. Write your daughters, granddaughters, or nieces a note, celebrating their awareness of their body's needs and their growing capacity to express and meet them. Write yourself a note of appreciation for the ways you nurture your own awareness of your body's needs and your capacity to express and meet them.

Childhood's Hurtful Words and Experiences

Eventually the awareness and expression of our natural needs were judged as fussy, needy, or "too sensitive" by our parents. They determined when we were cold or hot; when we were hungry; what foods were good for us; when, where and how we were to expel gas; and when they were available to hold us. They were the ones who determined if an expression of need was genuine or "manipulative." From early on, we received direct or indirect messages from our parents that it was not OK to have needs outside of the regulated and acceptable framework of family life, one usually based on their schedules.

Without the support of a "village" to assist them in raising us, our overwhelmed parents seldom consulted us about what we needed or didn't need. Instead, they tightened around any spontaneous expression of need, convincing us that something was wrong with our natural "neediness."

In an attempt to fit into home and school environments that did not honor the natural impulses of our developing bodies, we learned to ignore its needs and to develop the essential skill of conquering the body by "waiting" an hour to eat, "holding it" until bathroom time, or by censoring our desire to be touched. Compounding our deepening "disembodiedness," we were groomed to anticipate and then meet the physical needs of others in our training to become housewives and mothers. Preoccupied with the growing demands to service others, we ignored our own body's signals to stretch, to rest, to eat, or to

Unfortunately, most of us have become so alienated from our bodies that it is difficult to access our bodies' wisdom. This is a grave handicap. For body wisdom contains the essential truths about what matters most to a woman and ultimately to the human race as a whole. Body wisdom especially amplifies the inherent sacred relationship between a woman and the deep feminine. If she doubts this, she has but to turn to the exquisitely sensitive cycles of her body that have been teaching her since puberty how intimately she is influenced by the innate intelligence of her biochemical bodymind.

—Paula M. Reeves,
  Women's Intuition

go to the bathroom. Depleted, we lost touch with our own needs.

What words twisted your awareness and expression of your natural needs and impulses out of shape and encouraged the disembodied self? Note the words in your journal. Choose whichever activity moves you: Write a note to your parents, expressing anger, frustration, or disappointment that they did not support your capacity to be aware of, express, and meet your body's needs. Write a note to daughters, granddaughters, or nieces, acknowledging the ways you did not support their capacity to be aware of, express, and meet their body's needs.

Healing Words and Experiences

Participate in the "Healthy Family Fantasy" through play/drama or in the quietness of your healing imagination. Trust your own impulse to sit quietly or to enact the fantasy. Enter into a childhood hoped for. . . . Place your childhood name in the blank.

Sometimes your father reads to you from *The Book of Woman*. One school night after you finish your homework, he offers to read your favorite story, "_____'s Best Friend." He begins:

Our child-friendly fantasies and experiences settled into the ground of our being as seeds of promise, reminding us that things could be different and that our fantasies were not vain imaginings. In the fullness of time, they bear fruit in a healthy life in the present.

—PLR

_____'s body is her best friend. It's been telling her what she needs since she was a baby when others took care of all of her needs. Her body let her know what it needed and then she let the adults know by fussing and crying. When her body was cold, she cried and someone wrapped her up. When her body was hungry, she cried and someone fed her. When her diaper was wet, she cried and someone changed her.

Now that she can talk and walk, and doesn't wear a diaper, things have changed. Sometimes she uses words to let her family know what her body needs. When _____'s ears tell her that the music blaring from her sister's room is too loud, she asks her sister to please turn the music down or to wear her headphones. Sometimes no words are needed. She crawls onto her grandmother's lap when she needs to be held.

Most times _____ takes care of her own needs because she listens to her best friend. When she is tired, she falls asleep wherever she may be—in someone's arms . . . or on the department store floor. And when she doesn't get enough sleep, her body is a big blob all day and she can't do all the fun things she wants to because she feels like going back to sleep. On those days she needs a nap.

When _____'s body lets her know its hungry, she goes into the kitchen and gets a snack. When her body tells her that it's time to get rid of the stuff it doesn't need, she finds her way to the nearest bathroom. When _____'s body is satisfied at the end of a meal it burps to say, "Thank you." And when her sister says, "Well, excuse you," _____ says, "Its my body's way of saying thank you for a good meal." When her stomach isn't happy about the food she's eaten, like when she eats a turkey burger and cantaloupe for dessert, it farts. If she tries to be "polite" by holding the fart in, her stomach hurts really bad.

_____'s body tells her everything she needs to know. It even tells her when she likes someone and when she doesn't. Whenever her grandmother is coming over to visit, _____'s heart feels warm and her breath goes all the way down into her belly. One day her mother brought over a new friend of hers. As soon as he walked into their apartment, _____'s stomach got really tight so there was no room for her breath and said, "I don't like him." She whispered, "Thanks for telling me, Stomach." Then after the man left, _____'s told her mother what her stomach said. And lo and behold, her mother's stomach said the same thing. They never invited that man over again.

_____ and her grandmother play a secret game together whenever she visits her "Nana" in Connecticut. It's called "Listen to Your Best Friend!" They sit on the couch with their eyes closed. It is quiet, very quiet.

"Listen and tell me what you hear," Nana says.
"My stomach made a sound and the sound skipped up to my belly button," _____ answers.

"Listen and tell me what you hear," _____ says to her Nana.
"My breath is filling my belly and it is growing bigger and rounder like a balloon filled with air," Nana answers.

_____ and her Nana go back and forth listening and telling until their bodies want to get up and move around. When they are all finished, _____ always says to her Nana, "You are my second favorite best friend in the whole world." And Nana always asks, "Who's your first favorite best friend?" "I am my first favorite person in the whole wide world and my body is my first best friend." Nana always hugs _____ and says, "May it always be so, dear one."

Remember a childhood scene involving your capacity to express or to meet your body's needs. If your capacity was supported in the scene, write it as you remember it. If your capacity was not supported in the scene you remember, rewrite it. Enter into the scene with your healing imagination: replace all critical words and persons with supportive ones. If the "Healthy Family Fantasy" touched or inspired you, read it again and again. Using the "Listening to Your Best Friend" exercise as your inspiration, review your schedule and list possible dates and times to experience a weekly "listening to your body" meditation with your daughter . . . with yourself.

Descent and Rediscovery

Imagine yourself as a leaf let go of by an autumn tree . . . a leaf slowly and gradually descending toward the ground . . . its descent cushioned by the breath of life . . . a leaf touching the ground in the forest deep within your being. You rise from the ground, thanking the leaf for transporting you so gently.

Everything breathes in the forest. Savor the breath of life flowing in and around you. Inhale deeply as the breath rises from the rich earth beneath you. Release the breath into the cool and moist air around you. Your attention moves upward and you notice the trees reaching arm in arm for the sky. You become a tree. Your feet grow roots extending deep into the ground. Your arms become branches stretching high into the sky. You sway with the breeze. The birds of the forest dance with you as they leap from branch to branch. You see many things from your new height.

A nearby stream calls to you, "Come and play." In a moment, you are at the stream, splashing in its bouncing waters. As you are drying off in the warm sunlight pouring through the forest canopy, a path opens up before you and invites you to follow it to a special place. You accept the invitation and follow the path. The path leads you deep within the forest to the edge of a clearing . . . a magical open space surrounded by a ring of ancient redwoods, forming the outer circle, and by a sparkling stream, forming the inner circle. You cross the stream. You enter the clearing.

A woman approaches you: "The Mother of All Living is waiting. She has a gift for you. Come let us meet her in the center of the clearing." You see the Mother at a distance. You approach her with your arms at your sides. You feel no shame in her presence. Her eyes meet yours and in her gaze, you are recognized . . . shaken . . . and relieved. She embraces you and you become as you once were . . . fully present and in love with yourself. She hands you a beautifully wrapped gift. As you open it, she speaks, "Daughter of Woman, dance the sadness of a lifetime for what could never be. And when your sadness is quieted, dance with her partner, gladness. For as deep a cavern as sorrow has carved within you that shall be your capacity for joy. Dance your gladness for what is now and will be forevermore.

"Daughter of Woman, receive again your birthright. Listen to the sounds and sensations of a lifetime. You body is the bearer of deep wisdom. What does it tell you of the quality of your life, of the shape and pace of your days, of those who dance into and out of your presence, of the food you eat, of the sleep you embrace, of your response to the experiences of life? Listen to what you hear and meet your body's needs with tenderness and grace. The organic needs of the universe pulsate through you. Be full of yourself!"

Vow Faithfulness to Your Body's Organic Needs

Imagine a woman who trusts and respects herself. A woman who listens to her needs and desires. Who meets them with tenderness and grace. Imagine yourself as this woman . . . as you vow faithfulness to your body's needs.

Use the following activities to inspire, provoke, and give shape to your vow:

1. List the ways you listen to and meet your body's needs in your journal. If you are a parent, list the ways you nurture your daughter's capacity to listen to and meet her body's needs.

2. Create two columns in your journal. In column 1, list the present-day challenges/opposition to listening to and meeting your body's needs. In column 2, list the ways you will preserve allegiance to your body's needs against each challenge/opposition.

3. Imagine being asked the following questions in your ceremony of commitment. In your journal note the memories, feelings, and sensations triggered as you "hear" each question and as you imagine answering, "I Will."

> Will you listen to the deep wisdom of your body all the days of your life?
> Will you meet its needs with tenderness and grace?
> Will you design the shape of your days in accordance with its feedback?
> Will you eat foods that support its vitality, drink water to moisten its capacities, and sleep well to renew its life energy?

4. Allow women's vows to inspire your own. Highlight the phrases that resonate with your experience.

I will breathe into my belly.

I vow to treat myself to facials and pedicures monthly.

I will notice and accept my body's sensations as trustworthy information.

I vow to honor my body by what I choose to ingest and how I choose to be touched.

I will ask my body often, "Is this working for you?" and listen carefully for its answer.

I promise to befriend my body, to lovingly provide the nourishment, rest, and exercise it needs.

I promise to refrain from stuffing my body with more food than it can possibly use up; if I am full of myself, I will not need to be so full of food.

5. Take a deep breath. Gather phrases from the above exercises, sprinkle in some new ones, and compose a one- to three-sentence vow of faithfulness to your body's organic needs.

Step 2 Reclaim Your Sexual Autonomy

Remember Your Birthright

In the very beginning, the girl-child is acquainted with the erotic energy within her. From birth, she is capable of sexual arousal and orgasm. She says a big "Yes" to life as it pulsates through her. She feels the "Yes" in her curiosity about her body's sensations and in her exploration of its fascinating nooks and crannies, openings and operations. Her body is her closest friend. She discovers her clitoris and receives pleasure from touching it. She experiences her body's sensuality by feeling its smoothness and curves, by touching its lips, by entering its openings, by tasting its juiciness, and by delighting in its natural fragrances. She also feels the "Yes" in her heart, her joy, and even in her tears. It touches every area of her life. The erotic potential of the universe pulsates through her.

Pause to remember your original erotic potential: a time when you discovered something new and exciting about your body; a time when you touched your clitoris, delighting in your own body; a time when you were unashamed to look at yourself in the mirror with great joy. If you do not remember the very beginning, recall the times when you observed the erotic potential of your preadolescent daughter, granddaughter, or niece: the many times she pranced around the house naked, dancing joyously; a time when she wanted to stay in the bathtub for hours, playing with her body shamelessly. Allow your daughter, granddaughter, or niece to awaken memories of a time when you were full of yourself . . . in the very beginning of life.

Choose whichever activity moves you: Write your parents a note of appreciation for nurturing your sexual autonomy. Write your daughters, granddaughters, or nieces a note celebrating their sexual autonomy. Write yourself a note of appreciation for the ways you nurture your own sexual autonomy.

Childhood's Hurtful Words and Experiences

Eventually, our original erotic potential was judged as unfeminine, immodest, and impure by our parents' words and actions. For those of us who were touched affectionately by our parents, touch was seldom extended beyond early childhood. As we matured and grew out of the "cute stage," our parents became uncomfortable with our developing bodies and most touching stopped abruptly. We created stories to make sense of this withdrawal of affection. We became convinced that there was something wrong with our bodies, and that our

I have such a strong connection with my daughter. She reminds me of the girl child I once was. She is perfect. I look at her and I don't see any flaws. Everything I celebrate in her reminds me of my true nature. As I parent her in the way I wish I had been parented, the child in me is healed.
—ERIN LOUISE STEWART

growing breasts and pubic hair, and the new sensations we were experiencing in our genitals made us untouchable to our parents. For some of us, the incestuous behavior of a parent or relative compounded this growing discomfort.

Although in the very beginning of our lives we discovered the clitoris as a source of pleasure, we entered adolescence convinced that the vagina was our only sexual organ. It became the focus of sexual pleasure in a culture that reduced sexuality to genital intercourse and that defined sexuality according to the needs and desires of men. We were required to accept a form of sexuality that required a partner and that did not in and of itself offer us satisfaction. Because our early erotic autonomy was not cultivated by our parents, we eventually became ignorant of the mechanics of female sexuality and dependent on others to meet our needs. Groomed by our parents to service men sexually, we forgot about the wonders of our own bodies and their capacity for sensual delight and satisfaction. Our original love of the body, our curiosity about its sensations, and our exploration of its fascinating nooks and crannies, openings and operations were twisted out of shape and labeled unacceptable by our families . . . and by ourselves.

What words twisted your original erotic potential out of shape and cultivated the sexually passive self? Note the words in your journal. Choose whichever activity moves you: Write a note to your parents, expressing anger, frustration, or disappointment that they did not support your sexual autonomy to develop and flourish. Write a note to daughters, granddaughters, or nieces, acknowledging the ways you did not support their sexual autonomy to develop and flourish.

Healing Words and Experiences

Participate in the "Healthy Family Fantasy" through play/drama or in the quietness of your healing imagination. Trust your own impulse to sit quietly or to enact the fantasy. Enter into a childhood hoped for. . . .

> On a special night near your twelfth birthday, your mother and two of her special friends meet you at the altar in your room. On the altar are pictures of those you love, a container with the ashes of your grandmother's body, a red candle and scarf, and the special *Book of Woman* given to you by your parents when you were very young. Your mother reads as you listen.

> I am Woman. I stride the Earth in nakedness.

> No robes hide the beauty of my fertile womb, my rounded belly, and my full breasts.

> I am She Who Is Complete in Herself.

> I live in my body. I embrace its desires as my own.

> Daughter of Woman, the Goddesses loved themselves to their edges.

> Self-possessed, they strode the earth. Women full of themselves.

> Embracing their sexuality as their own. Delighting in pleasuring themselves.

> Experiencing all their erotic feelings and sensations without shame.

> Daughter of Woman, own yourself completely.

> Embark on an intimate journey into yourself.

> Connect with the whole and complete center within you.

> Experience fullness, self-possession, and satisfaction.

Delight in your freedom to be alone.

To meet your own needs. To give yourself pleasure.

Daughter of Woman, your body is your own. It is no one else's.

Live in your body. Trusts its natural instincts.

Experience the pleasure of your body's sensuality.

Feel its smoothness and its curves. Touch its lips. Enter its openings.

Taste its juiciness. Delight in its natural fragrances.

Explore the edges of your sensuality.

Daughter of Woman, feel the fire awaken within you.

Fire rising from the depths. Lover uncoiling to meet lover.

Height calling to depth. Earth moving toward heaven.

Celebrate the sensations in your genitals.

They are calling you to your edges.

Daughter of Woman, all the feelings in your body are good.

The tingling. The pulsations of pleasure. The swelling to overflowing.

Honor all that has been demeaned.

Receive all that has been cast aside.

Your mother asks you questions: "Have you ever felt the fiery warmth rise in your body? Where did these feelings begin? Where did they end? Have you ever felt a tingling sensation in your genitals? Did these feelings scare or excite you?" Your mother and her friends answer the questions too. And then your mother says to you, "It is so very good for you to touch your own body. To explore its smoothness and curves. To open its lips. To enter its openings. Anyone else—other than you—must ask your permission to touch, hug, or hold you. Your 'No' must be respected as highly as your 'Yes.'"

After you finish the conversation, you trace each other's bodies on big pieces of newsprint. And then you each draw the fiery warmth and the tingling sensations you feel in special places on your own bodies, using red, yellow, and orange paint and all different colors of glitter. Afterward you talk about your drawings.

Pause to remember a scene from childhood involving your sexuality. If your sexuality was supported in the scene, write it as you remember it. If your sexuality was not supported in the scene you remember, rewrite it . Enter into the scene with your healing imagination: replace all critical words and persons with supportive ones. If the "Healthy Family Fantasy" touched you, read it again and again.

Descent and Rediscovery

Imagine yourself as a leaf let go of by an autumn tree . . . a leaf slowly and gradually descending toward the ground . . . its descent cushioned by the breath of life . . . a leaf touching the ground in the forest deep within your being. You rise from the ground, thanking the leaf for transporting you so gently.

Everything breathes in the forest. Savor the breath of life flowing in and around you. Inhale deeply as the breath rises from the rich earth beneath you. Release the breath into the cool and moist air around you. Your attention moves upward, and you notice the trees reaching arm in arm for the sky. You become a tree. Your feet grow roots extending deep into the ground. Your arms become branches stretching high into the sky. You sway with the breeze. The birds of the forest dance with you as they leap from branch to branch. You see many things from your new height.

A nearby stream calls to you, "Come and play." In a moment, you are at the stream, splashing in its bouncing waters. As you are drying off in the warm sunlight pouring through the forest canopy, a path opens up before you and invites you to follow it to a special place. You accept the invitation and follow the path. The path leads you deep within the forest to the edge of a clearing . . . a magical open space surrounded by a ring of ancient redwoods, forming the outer circle, and by a sparkling stream, forming the inner circle. You cross the stream. You enter the clearing.

A woman approaches you: "The Mother of All Living is waiting. She has a gift for you. Come let us meet her in the center of the clearing." You see the Mother at a distance. You approach her with your arms at your sides. You feel no shame in her presence. Her eyes meet yours and in her gaze, you are recognized . . . shaken . . . and relieved. She embraces you and you become as you once were . . . fully present and in love with yourself. She hands you a beautifully wrapped gift. As you open it, she speaks, "Daughter of Woman, dance the sadness of a lifetime for what could never be. And when your sadness is quieted, dance with her partner, gladness. For as deep a cavern as sorrow has carved within you that shall be your capacity for joy. Dance your gladness for what is now and will be forevermore.

"Daughter of Woman, receive again your birthright. Say 'Yes' . . . to life as it pulsates through you. Feel the 'Yes' in your curiosity about your body's

When we begin to live from within outward, in touch with the power of the erotic within ourselves, then we begin to be responsible to ourselves in the deepest sense. For as we recognize our deepest feelings, we begin to give up, of necessity, being satisfied with suffering and self-negation, and the numbness which so often seems like the only alternative in our society.

—AUDRE LORDE,
SISTER OUTSIDER

154

sensations and in your exploration of its fascinating nooks and crannies, openings and operations. Feel the 'Yes' in your heart, your joy, and even in your tears. Allow it to touch every area of your life. The erotic potential of the universe pulsates through you. Be full of yourself."

Vow Faithfulness to Your Sexuality

Imagine a woman who embraces her sexuality as her own. A woman who delights in pleasuring herself. Who experiences her erotic feelings and sensations without shame or guilt. Imagine yourself as this woman as you vow faithfulness to sexuality.

Use the following activities to inspire, provoke, and give shape to your vow:

1. List the ways you nurture your relationship to your sexuality in your journal. If you are a parent, list the ways you nurture your daughter's relationship to her sexuality.

2. Create two columns in your journal. In column 1, list the present-day challenges/opposition to maintaining your relationship to your sexuality. In column 2, list the ways you will preserve allegiance to your sexuality against each challenge/opposition.

3. In your journal, note the memories, feelings, and sensations that are triggered as you read each of the following questions and as you imagine answering "I Will" in a ceremony of commitment to yourself.

Will you embrace your sexuality as your own all the days of
   your life?
Will you delight in pleasuring yourself?
Will you explore the edges of your sensuality?
Will you trust your body's clear "Yes" and "No" in the choice
   of lovers?

4. Allow women's vows to inspire your own. Highlight the phrases
   that resonate with your experience.

   I vow to trust my sexuality and savor my sensuality.

   I vow to honor my body by how I choose to be touched.

   I will take care of my body and make time for sensual pleasure.

   I will ask my body often, "Is this working for you?" and listen carefully for its answer.

   I vow to own, explore, and celebrate my sexuality as a vital, natural, and healthy resource.

5. Take a deep breath. Gather phrases from the above exercises,
   sprinkle in some new ones, and compose a one- to three-
   sentence vow of faithfulness to your sexuality.

Step 4 Reclaim Your Expression of the Full Range of Emotion

Remember Your Birthright

In the very beginning, the girl-child has the capacity to feel and to express the
whole range of human emotion. It is through her body that she knows her

feelings, and it is through movement and sound that she releases the energy that accompanies each feeling. There is no separation between her feelings and her body. They are one within her. She feels sadness as an ache in her heart and as the tears flowing from her eyes. She feels anger rise up within her to be released in loud sounds and strong movements. She feels fear in the shortness of her breath and in the fluttering sensation in her tummy. She feels erotic energy in the tingling warmth of her genitals. She feels joy in the warmth of her face, the smile in her eyes, and in the giggle inside of her. Her feelings ebb and flow as naturally as the breath. When she gets angry, she stomps and yells, and before you know it, she's smiling and off with a friend. The expression of a full range of human emotion is essential to her physical and psychological health. Her immune system is strengthened by the circulation of her feelings. The feelings of the universe pulsate through her.

Pause to remember your original awareness and expression of the whole range of human emotion: a time when you were angry and felt it pass through your body and then be gone; a time when your heart ached and you felt comforted as you cried into your pillow; a time when you were happy, sad, and angry within one day and it was OK.

If you do not remember the very beginning, recall your preadolescent daughter, granddaughter, or niece's ability to express her feelings: a time when she let it be known that she was angry at her brother for entering her room without permission; a time when she needed to talk about her absent father with tears in her eyes while pounding her fist into a

On a daily basis, I affirm the goodness of my body. This ongoing affirmation is essential because I'm bombarded by images of the perfect body and by messages that my life will be perfect if I just lose 10 pounds. The daily assault on my body is painful. More often than not, I am completely happy with my body, its feelings and sexuality, and how it looks as well. In this healed frame of mind, I don't want to change a thing. I don't want to begin a new exercise or diet regimen. I want to go on living.
—COLLEEN WEST

nearby pillow. Allow your daughter, granddaughter, or niece to awaken memories of a time when you were in touch with all your feelings.

Choose whichever activity moves you: Write your parents a note of appreciation for nurturing your awareness and expression of the whole range of human emotion. Write your daughters, granddaughters, or nieces a note celebrating their awareness and expression of the whole range of human emotion. Write yourself a note of appreciation for the ways you nurture your own awareness and expression of the whole range of human emotion.

Childhood's Hurtful Words and Experiences

For most of us, our capacity to feel was judged as fickle and too intense by our parents. Although we were allowed more room to feel than our brothers, there was an inherent judgment surrounding our capacity to feel. We learned that feelings were not as important as thoughts and that boys think while girls feel. Our feelings were tolerated at best and dismissed as evidence of our inferiority at worst. We heard rumors of women whose feelings kept them from getting the job done, unlike men who mastered their feelings and completed the task at hand; of women who were too emotional and good for nothing especially at "that time of the month," unlike men who could be counted on all the time; of women who were fickle, erratic, and unstable because they let their feelings get the best of them, unlike men who were reliable and controlled.

> *If we breathe deeply,*
> *feeling erupts,*
> *grows too intense for us.*
> *So we keep our breath shallow.*
> *To breathe deeply*
> *is to receive and that is the feminine incarnate.*
> —MARION WOODMAN,
> COMING HOME TO MYSELF

We were taught that there are good feelings and bad feelings. Responsible for the reactions of others, we began to sort through our feelings. Bad feelings were to be controlled and kept inside because they made others uncomfortable. Good feelings could be expressed as long as they weren't too intense. Intensity made everyone uncomfortable. We became aware of boy-feelings and girl-feelings. Girls got hurt and cried a lot. Boys got angry and yelled a lot. If a boy got hurt, he was called a "sissy." If a girl got angry, she was called "unfeminine" and "ugly." Humble, discreet, and considerate, we learned to cry when we were angry and to smile when we really wanted to yell.

What words convinced you of the inferiority of your capacity to feel; required you to categorize feelings into good/bad, and girl/boy compartments; and allowed only the expression of "acceptable" emotions? Note the words in your journal. Choose whichever activity moves you: Write a note to your parents, expressing anger, frustration, or disappointment that they did not support your awareness and expression of the whole range of human emotion. Write a note to daughters, granddaughters, or nieces, acknowledging the ways you did not support their awareness and expression of the whole range of human emotion.

Healing Words and Experiences

Participate in the "Healthy Family Fantasy" however it suits you. Trust your own impulse to sit quietly or to enact the fantasy. Enter into a childhood hoped for....

> You return home after saying good-bye to your best friend Amy, whose family has just moved away to a new neighborhood in another state. You are crying because she was your very best friend and you will miss her. You spent every waking hour together, making things and inventing new projects to do with the kids in the neighborhood. Your mom and dad invite

you to sit between them on the couch in the living room. They each take a hand and in the silence; you cry. Your father says, "Your tears are so lovely. Your sadness touches my heart." Your mother squeezes your hand gently. You look up and there are tears in both their eyes as you sit together in the comforting silence. You cry until the tears stop all by themselves and until the sadness doesn't hurt so much in your heart.

"Does your sadness have anything to say?" your father asks.

"No, there is nothing to say right now."

"Does your sadness want to dance?" asks your mother.

"No, it is quiet now. Maybe later."

"Does your sadness have a color?"

"Yes, let's draw. You draw too. Remember a time when you were very sad and draw with me."

Together you gather the special markers, the ones like paintbrushes used only to express feelings. You each draw your sadness. Afterward you talk about your drawing: "My picture is the color blue. Amy's favorite color. She wore it all the time. The blue is going away to the other neighborhood. And there is a little bit of blue left behind in everyone's heart. See there's blue in my heart because that's where she will stay."

It is always important for us to be aware of our feelings. Our feelings exist for good reason and so deserve our attention and respect. Even uncomfortable feelings that we might prefer to avoid, such as anger and depression, may serve to preserve the dignity and integrity of the self.
—HARRIET GOLDHOR LERNER,
THE DANCE OF INTIMACY

Your dad and mom drew their sadness because they will miss Amy too. Dad remembered all the times Amy spent the night. He could hear you and Amy whispering until very late. And he would smile, so very happy you had a special friend who loved you. Mom always set a place for her at dinner whether she was with us or not. "Can we still do it, Mom?" "Sure," she says.

And so it happens: every day for many months an extra place is set at the table for Amy until the day in June when she comes to visit for a week and sits at your table as she once did. Everyone smiles.

Pause to remember a scene from childhood involving your awareness or expression of emotion. If your feeling capacity was supported in the scene, write it as you remember it. If your feeling capacity was not supported in the scene you remember, rewrite it. Enter into the scene with your healing imagination: replace all critical words and persons with supportive ones. If the "Healthy Family Fantasy" touched or inspired you, read it again and again. Using it as your inspiration, create a family or personal ritual to honor the whole range of human emotion.

Descent and Rediscovery

Imagine yourself as a leaf let go of by an autumn tree . . . a leaf slowly and gradually descending toward the ground . . . its descent cushioned by the breath of life . . . a leaf touching the ground in the forest deep within your being. You rise from the ground, thanking the leaf for transporting you so gently.

Everything breathes in the forest. Savor the breath of life flowing in and around you. Inhale deeply as the breath rises from the rich earth beneath you. Release the breath into the cool and moist air

Raise your daughters with emotional integrity by helping them to be emotionally real to themselves and others. Honor all of her expressions of feeling. When she is a baby, this means understanding that she has to cry and fuss as she adjusts to her new world. When she is a toddler, it means knowing that her tantrums are a legitimate venting of her frustration—she is expressing herself in a healthy way. When she is a preteen and begins to withdraw from you or express anger toward you, it means understanding that she needs to separate from you as she moves toward adolescence.

—Virginia Beane Rutter,
Celebrating Girls

around you. Your attention moves upward and you notice the trees reaching arm in arm for the sky. You become a tree. Your feet grow roots extending deep into the ground. Your arms become branches stretching high into the sky. You sway with the breeze. The birds of the forest dance with you as they leap from branch to branch. You see many things from your new height.

A nearby stream calls to you, "Come and play." In a moment, you are at the stream, splashing in its bouncing waters. As you are drying off in the warm sunlight pouring through the forest canopy, a path opens up before you and invites you to follow it to a special place. You accept the invitation and follow the path. The path leads you deep within the forest to the edge of a clearing . . . a magical open space surrounded by a ring of ancient redwoods, forming the outer circle, and by a sparkling stream, forming the inner circle. You cross the stream. You enter the clearing.

A woman approaches you: "The Mother of All Living is waiting. She has a gift for you. Come let us meet her in the center of the clearing." You see the Mother at a distance. You approach her with your arms at your sides. You feel no shame in her presence. Her eyes meet yours and in her gaze, you are recognized . . . shaken . . . and relieved. She embraces you and you become as you once were . . . fully present and in love with yourself. She hands you a beautifully wrapped gift. As you open it, she speaks, "Daughter of Woman, dance the sadness of a lifetime for what could never be. And when your sadness is quieted, dance with her partner, gladness. For as deep a cavern as sorrow has carved within you that shall be your capacity for joy. Dance your gladness for what is now and will be forevermore.

"Daughter of Woman, receive again your birthright. No separation exists between your feelings and your body. They are one within you. Feel your sadness as an ache in your heart and as the tear flowing from your eyes. Feel your anger rise up within you to be released in loud sounds and strong movements.

Feel your fear in the shortness of your breath and in the fluttering sensation in your tummy. Feel your erotic energy in the tingling warmth of your genitals. Feels your joy in the warmth of your face, the smile in your eyes, and in the giggle inside of you. The feelings of the universe pulsate through you as naturally as the breath. Be full of yourself."

A Vow of Faithfulness to Your Emotions

Imagine a woman who has access to the full range of human emotion. A woman who expresses her feelings clearly and directly. Who allows them to pass through her as gracefully as the breath. Imagine yourself as this woman as you vow faithfulness to yourself.

Use the following activities to inspire, provoke, and give shape to your vow:

1. List the ways you nurture your relationship to your emotions in your journal. If you are a parent, list the ways you nurture your daughter's relationship to her emotions.

2. Create two columns in your journal. In column 1, list the present-day challenges/opposition to nurturing your relationship to your emotions. In column 2, list the ways you will preserve allegiance to your emotions against each challenge/opposition.

3. In your journal note the memories, feelings, and sensations that are triggered as you read each of the following questions and as you imagine answering, "I Will" at your own commitment ceremony.

> Will you honor the whole range of human emotion all the days of your life?

Will you circulate your feelings daily, using sound, movement, and image, allowing them to pass through you as
gracefully as the breath?

Will you take responsibility for meeting your own emotional
needs, enlisting the support of respectful friends and chosen family?

4. Allow women's vows to inspire your own. Highlight the phrases
that resonate with your experience.

I vow to honor the inherent validity of all my feelings.

I will allow myself to do or to not do simply because it feels right
and true to me.

I will feel all my feelings and not minimize or block them. I will
express them as I feel them.

I will honor that I am capable of feeling and expressing a full spec-
trum of human emotion.

5. Take a deep breath. Gather phrases from the above exercises,
sprinkle in some new ones, and compose a one- to three-
sentence vow of faithfulness to your emotions.

Step 5 Reclaim Your Capacity to Speak Your Truth

Remember Your Birthright

In the very beginning, the girl-child tells the truth about what she thinks and
how she responds to the events of life. She is transparent, forthright, and bold.

When she doesn't like her food, she spits it out. When she's exhausted from tagging along on a shopping spree, she refuses to take another step. When she doesn't like someone, she tightens in their presence and makes her discomfort known. She has a mind of her own and responds to the events of life with her own set of opinions. She tells her mother, "I get tired when you stay at those meetings so late. Can't we leave earlier?" She tells her father, "I like it when you read stories with me in the morning." She confronts her parents: "When you fight with each other late at night, I hear your voices and it makes me sad and afraid. I wish you wouldn't fight." She tells the truth when she is asked questions. The truth of the universe pulsates through her.

Pause to remember your original capacity to tell the truth and to trust your own perceptions and thoughts: The time when you let your mother know it was *not* OK that your grandfather did not ask permission before he hugged you; the time when you told the grouchy neighbor that it was *not* OK to yell at little children; or the time when you requested that your father keep his promise and spend more time with you on the weekends.

If you do not remember your childhood, recall your preadolescent daughter, granddaughter, or niece's ability to tell the truth and to trust her own perceptions: the time when she let you know that your hurried response to her question was not acceptable to her; or the time when she told you that she didn't like the man you were dating and listed the reasons why. Allow your daughter, granddaughter, or niece to awaken memories of a time when you were in touch with your own truth.

Choose whichever activity moves you: Write your parents a note of appreciation for nurturing your capacity to tell the truth and to trust your own

As a woman descends into the richness of her own life, she discovers the way home to herself. In the descent, she reverses the tendency to look outside of herself for salvation. In the "deep places," she reunites with her essential self and reclaims her natural capacities.
—PLR

perceptions and thoughts. Write your daughters, granddaughters, or nieces a note celebrating their capacity to tell the truth and to trust your own perceptions and thoughts. Write yourself a note of appreciation for the ways you nurture your own capacity to tell the truth and to trust your own perceptions and thoughts.

Childhood's Hurtful Words and Experiences

Eventually, our capacity to tell the truth was judged as rude and "not nice," and our capacity to think for ourselves as "troublesome" and "rocking the boat" by our families. We learned to question our own thoughts and perceptions and to lie in a compliance-based environment that valued conformity to outdated gender stereotypes and "politeness" more than it did integrity. We kept our thoughts about the events of life to ourselves so there wouldn't be an argument. We strained to like everyone so we wouldn't hurt anyone's feelings. We pretended that we didn't know what we knew so their egos wouldn't be hurt; that we didn't hear what we heard so their secrets wouldn't be exposed; and that we couldn't do what we could do so the masquerade about who was weak and who was strong would be maintained. The constant repetition of these childhood commandments censored our natural tendency to tell the truth and to think for ourselves. We learned to question our truth and to defer to the thoughts and perceptions of others, assuming something was wrong with us.

What words convinced you of the inferiority of your perceptions and thoughts; required you to categorize them into acceptable and unacceptable compartments; and allowed the expression of only acceptable ones. Note the words in your journal. Choose whichever activity moves you: Write a note to your parents, expressing anger, frustration, or disappointment that they did not support you to tell the truth and to trust your own perceptions and thoughts. Write a note to daughters, granddaughters, or nieces acknowledging the ways you did not support their capacity to tell the truth and to trust their own perceptions and thoughts.

Healing Words and Experiences

Participate in the "Healthy Family Fantasy" in the quietness of your healing imagination. Trust your own impulse to sit quietly or to enact the fantasy. Enter into a childhood hoped for. . . .

> Your mother calls you and your sisters together for a family meeting. She begins with a reading from *The Book of Woman:* "For Mother God so loved the world that she sent into its midst the Divine Girl-Child. Whosoever believes in Her goodness, listens to Her wisdom, and celebrates Her power will be awakened to the abundance of gifts within them."
>
> "I have called this meeting to discuss a new job I have been offered. Whatever decision is made will effect all of us so I want to lay out the situation and hear your concerns." She then lists the benefits of the new job: Weekends off. Better health benefits. Paid two-week vacation. Then she lays out the challenges of the job: After-school care until 6 P.M. every day. Less time with her during the week. Long days for everyone from Monday to Friday.
>
> Each of the children has a turn to express her opinion about the changes. You respond, "The kids are wild after school and I don't like to be around them for three hours. The child care people are not as good with kids as the teachers. I'd rather go to Aunt Lucy's than stay at school." Your mother

asks you how many days you can handle staying at school. "Three days," you say, "because there is drama class after school on Monday-Wednesday-Friday and I like drama."

"OK," Mom responds, "we'll call Aunt Lucy and see if she can pick you up on Tuesdays and Thursdays."

"I have two more problems. First off, I get really hungry after school and the snack is not enough." Your mother asks, "Would it work for you to make two lunches for yourself on Monday-Wednesday-Friday and eat one after school?"

"Good idea. My other problem is that I want to be sure that we really do get to do fun things on the weekend when you are off. Not just laundry and stuff to clean up around the house."

"OK," your mom responds, "Let's plan a date for every Saturday evening. We'll go roller skating or we'll rent a movie. No chores or busyness on Saturday from 5 P.M. on. How's that?" "Now that we've worked through all that stuff, I vote 'Yes' to your new job."

Your mom thanks you for being so clear about what doesn't work for you. "It's fun to co-create solutions with you. You have great ideas and I can always count on you to tell me the truth about things even if it's a hard truth. Thank you!"

Pause to remember a scene from childhood involving your capacity to tell the truth and to trust your own perceptions and thoughts. If your capacity was supported in the scene, write it as you remember it. If your capacity was not supported in the scene you remember, rewrite it. Enter into the scene with your healing imagination: replace all critical words and persons with supportive ones. If the "Healthy Family Fantasy" touched or inspired you, read it again and again. Using it as your inspiration, incorporate a family or relationship meeting into your weekly schedule at which each person's truth will be listened to and acknowledged.

Descent and Rediscovery

Imagine yourself as a leaf let go of by an autumn tree . . . a leaf slowly and gradually descending toward the ground . . . its descent cushioned by the breath of life . . . a leaf touching the ground in the forest deep within your being. You rise from the ground, thanking the leaf for transporting you so gently.

Everything breathes in the forest. Savor the breath of life flowing in and around you. Inhale deeply as the breath rises from the rich earth beneath you. Release the breath into the cool and moist air around you. Your attention moves upward and you notice the trees reaching arm in arm for the sky. You become a tree. Your feet grow roots extending deep into the ground. Your arms become branches stretching high into the sky. You sway with the breeze. The birds of the forest dance with you as they leap from branch to branch. You see many things from your new height.

A nearby stream calls to you, "Come and play." In a moment, you are at the stream, splashing in its bouncing waters. As you are drying off in the warm sunlight pouring through the forest canopy, a path opens up before you and invites you to follow it to a special place. You accept the invitation and follow the path. The path leads you deep within the forest to the edge of a clearing . . . a magical open space surrounded by a ring of ancient redwoods, forming the outer

To step outside of patriarchal thought means: . . . overcoming the deep-seated resistance within ourselves toward accepting ourselves and our knowledge as valid. It means getting rid of the great men in our heads and substituting for them ourselves, our sisters, our anonymous foremothers.

—GERDA LERNER,
THE CREATION OF PATRIARCHY

circle, and by a sparkling stream, forming the inner circle. You cross the stream. You enter the clearing.

A woman approaches you: "The Mother of All Living is waiting. She has a gift for you. Come let us meet her in the center of the clearing." You see the Mother at a distance. You approach her with your arms at your sides. You feel no shame in her presence. Her eyes meet yours and in her gaze, you are recognized . . . shaken . . . and relieved. She embraces you and you become as you once were . . . fully present and in love with yourself. She hands you a beautifully wrapped gift. As you open it, she speaks, "Daughter of Woman, dance the sadness of a lifetime for what could never be. And when your sadness is quieted, dance with her partner, gladness. For as deep a cavern as sorrow has carved within you that shall be your capacity for joy. Dance your gladness for what is now and will be forevermore.

"Daughter of Woman, be sassy and loud. Question. Argue. Debate. Communicate from your heart. Voice your truth. Share your vision. When you don't like your food, spit it out. When you're exhausted from tagging along in someone else's life, refuse to take another step. When you don't like someone and tighten in their presence, make your discomfort known. Tell the untold truths of a lifetime to your parents, lovers, and colleagues, and to your children and grandchildren. The truth of the universe pulsates through you. Be full of yourself!"

A Vow of Faithfulness to Your Truth

Imagine a woman who tells the truth. A woman who trusts her experience of the world and expresses it. Who refuses to defer to the thoughts, perceptions, and responses of others. Imagine yourself as this woman as you vow faithfulness to your truth.

Use the following activities to inspire, provoke, and give shape to your vow:

1. List the ways you nurture your capacity to tell the truth and to trust your perceptions and thoughts in your journal. If you are a parent, list the ways you nurture your daughter's capacity to tell the truth and to trust your perceptions and thoughts.

2. Create two columns in your journal. In column 1, list the present-day challenges/opposition to maintaining your capacity to tell the truth and trust your perceptions and thoughts. In column 2, list the ways you will preserve allegiance to your truth against each challenge/opposition.

3. In your journal note the memories, feelings, and sensations that come up as you read each of the following questions and as you imagine answering, "I Will" in your own commitment ceremony.

   Will you speak your truth all the days of your life?
   Will you tell the untold truths of a lifetime to your parents, lovers, and colleagues, and to your children and grand children?
   Will you assume intellectual equality by refusing to defer to the thoughts and perceptions of others?

4. Allow women's vows to inspire your own. Highlight the phrases that resonate with your experience.

   I will speak in a voice clear and strong.

I vow to assertively state what I think and feel.

I vow to listen for my inner truth and then speak it.

I will be willing to not only speak the truth but also to hear the truth.

I vow to act courageously in speaking my truths as loudly or as softly as they need to be spoken.

I will state clearly when something doesn't work for me and co-create an acceptable alternative.

5. Take a deep breath. Gather phrases from the above exercises, sprinkle in some new ones, and compose a one- to three-sentence vow of faithfulness to your truth.

Step 6 Reclaim Your Solitude

Remember Your Birthright

In the very beginning, the girl-child enjoys the privacy of quiet times, under-the-cover times, alone times, to digest the experiences of her life. She is always available to herself, so she is never really alone. She keeps some things to herself, holding them in the privacy of her own heart. She has a new idea that's too fragile to share so she keeps it close to her. If she tells someone about it too soon, the fragile blossom may wilt from premature exposure. She has a new friend who's too new to invite into her very private dreams; theirs is still too fragile a connection to hold the fullness of who she is. She has a new relationship with her body as it changes from day to day. She needs private time to befriend each change before she exposes her body to others. She loves the quiet of the night when everything slows down and she has a chance to think about the day, to feel the sadness in her heart, to let her imagination drift to other worlds, to see the dancing images of her night dreams—all by herself. The solitude of the universe pulsates through her.

In the very beginning, the girl-child is interested in herself and involved in self-motivated adventures. She is a natural explorer of everything in her world. Her ordinary life is interesting enough. Every experience is filled with wonder. It is enough to gaze at the redness of an apple; to watch the water flow over the rocks in a stream; to listen to the rain dance; to count the peas on her plate. Ordinary life is her teacher, her challenge, and her delight. She is never bored. There is always another adventure and project to turn toward. Only on her terms does she want to share a luscious piece of her grandma's cake or a seashell from her chest of special treasures or the letter her favorite aunt wrote to her from Africa. Much of the time, she wants to savor the pleasures of her own life all by herself. The vitality of the universe pulsates through her.

Pause to remember your self-interest and self-involvement: the time you sang songs to yourself for an hour straight without interruption, loving your own company; or the time when you ventured into the meadow beside your house in the morning and forgot all about lunch as you carried on important conversations with your favorite trees.

If you do not remember your childhood, recall the self-interest and self-involvement of your preadolescent daughter, granddaughter, or niece: the time when she put a sign on her door that read, "Do not disturb for the whole day. Please leave meals outside door." Allow your daughter, granddaughter, or niece to awaken memories of a time when you loved your solitude.

Choose whichever activity moves you: Write your parents a note of appreciation for nurturing your self-interest and self-involvement. Write your daughters, granddaughters, or nieces a note celebrating their self-interest and involvement. Write yourself a note of appreciation for the ways you nurture your self-interest and self-involvement.

Childhood's Hurtful Words and Experiences

Our natural self-interest was judged as selfish and self-centered by our families. Nice girls share their cake and treasures. Nice girls include others in their adventures. Nice girls don't hurt the feelings of others. "If you have a piece of chocolate cake and your friend doesn't, she will feel bad, so be sure to share." "If you are working on a project and your little brother wants to help, be sure to include him so he won't feel left out." We were required to share at the expense of our own healthy self-interest and to include others at the expense of our own healthy self-involvement. Our healthy narcissism and self-centeredness became crushed under the weight of these conformity-based expectations.

Our natural need for privacy was judged as selfish and unhelpful. We watched our mother closely and learned that she had no private time except maybe in the bathroom, but even there, someone was always barging in with a question or an emergency. Someone was always barging into our lives too. Barging in on our thoughts: "What are you thinking, young lady?" Barging into our feelings: "Why so sad today?" Barging in on our rooms: "The guests will stay in your room for the week. You will have to move into your sister's room." Barging in on our time: "I need Mama's helper to baby-sit your

It is essential for us to acknowledge childhood's hurtful words and experiences. We hold every memory, impression, image, word, event, and formative belief of childhood within us. Nothing has been lost or forgotten. It is impossible to ignore the past. It will always make itself known in troubling physical symptoms and persistent ineffective behaviors. In order to be an effective and responsible agent of transformation in the culture, we must walk through our personal past.

—PLR

little brother today." Barging in on our bodies: "Come and sit on my lap, pretty girl."

Someone was always barging in on our privacy with demands to help in the kitchen or to fix our little sister's hair. Our brother wasn't "on call" like we were. There were long stretches of time when he had nothing to do except what he wanted to do. His time was his own. Our time belonged to others. We were required to be helpful at the expense of our own healthy need for private time and space. The constant repetition of this childhood commandment censored our natural desire for solitude. Sometimes we felt like screaming, "Leave me alone!" Helpful and compliant, we swallowed those words and twisted our natural introversion into a much more acceptable and helper-oriented extroversion.

What words twisted your natural introversion into a more acceptable and helper-oriented extroversion? Note the words in your journal. Choose whichever activity moves you: Write a note to your parents, expressing anger, frustration, or disappointment that they did not support your self-interest and self-involvement. Write a note to daughters, granddaughters, or nieces acknowledging the ways you did not support their self-interest and self-involvement.

Healing Words and Experiences

Participate in the "Healthy Family Fantasy." Enter into a childhood hoped for.... Fill in the blanks based on your childhood family.

> Your mother calls your family together for the weekly family meeting. She asks you to read the "Family Code of Responsibility:"

The Responsibilities of All Family Members

1. We are a family made up of _____ members: _____ parents, _____ sister, and _____ brother. Each member is responsible to support the family to run smoothly and to help each other out when any challenges come along.

2. The parents are responsible to bring in the money to pay for the basic functioning of our family. This includes: rent to keep a roof over our heads; food to keep us alive; utilities to keep the water, heat, and electricity flowing; gasoline, maintenance, and insurance to keep our car in working order; fees for garbage pick-up; and the basic supplies necessary to keep a family going: from housecleaning and personal hygiene supplies to furniture and yard equipment.

3. The children are responsible to attend school to develop their minds and abilities. They will: prepare their school clothes; make their lunches; do their homework; and plan transportation to and from extracurricular events, clubs, and activities before 7 P.M. Monday through Friday.

4. All family members share the responsibility for house and yard chores. Everyone is responsible for their own room and bathroom. There are no girl-chores and boy-chores, no mommy-chores and daddy-chores. Each family member picks one daily, one weekly, and one extra chore to do for a month. If the children agree to do any chores over and above these basic responsibilities, they will be paid at a rate of $5 per hour.

The Privacy of All Family Members

1. Each family member has weekly private time. We will not barge in on another family member's privacy. We will guard and protect their pri-

vate time as they will protect ours. All questions and concerns for
them must wait until their private time is over.

Parent Private Time: _____ at _____ o'clock through _____ o'clock.

Parent Private Time: _____ at _____ o'clock through _____ o'clock.

Child Private Time: _____ at _____ o'clock through _____ o'clock.

Child Private Time: _____ at _____ o'clock through _____ o'clock.

2. Each family member is entitled to the privacy of their own thoughts
   and feelings, their own room, and their own body. We respect each
   other's "Yes"es and "No"s.

The Family Commitment

We are a family.

Together, we will find our way through each challenge we face. Together,
we will find a middle space between our differences. Together, we will
find a meeting place beyond right or wrong. Together, we will find a
comfortable way to live together that brings us all joy. May our family
blossom like a garden, one day at a time.

Pause to remember a scene from childhood involving your privacy and solitude. If your privacy and solitude were supported in the scene, write it as you remember it. If they were not supported in the scene you remember, rewrite it. Enter into the scene with your healing imagination: replace all critical words and persons with supportive ones. If the "Healthy Family Fantasy" touched or inspired you, read it again and again. Using it as your inspiration, develop a "Family Code of Responsibility."

We women have the abilities of a master juggler. We can survive while keeping a heroic number of balls in the air, but do we really thrive while doing so? Yes, if we also make room for plenty of silence in which meaning and wisdom can truly bloom. Blessings will flow to us when nurtured in refreshing solitude.
—SUE PATTON THOELE,
THE WOMAN'S BOOK OF SOUL

Descent and Rediscovery

Imagine yourself as a leaf let go of by an autumn tree . . . a leaf slowly and gradually descending toward the ground . . . its descent cushioned by the breath of life . . . a leaf touching the ground in the forest deep within your being. You rise from the ground, thanking the leaf for transporting you so gently.

Everything breathes in the forest. Savor the breath of life flowing in and around you. Inhale deeply as the breath rises from the rich earth beneath you. Release the breath into the cool and moist air around you. Your attention moves upward and you notice the trees reaching arm in arm for the sky. You become a tree. Your feet grow roots extending deep into the ground. Your arms become branches stretching high into the sky. You sway with the breeze. The birds of the forest dance with you as they leap from branch to branch. You see many things from your new height.

A nearby stream calls to you, "Come and play." In a moment, you are at the stream, splashing in its bouncing waters. As you are drying off in the warm sunlight pouring through the forest canopy, a path opens up before you and invites you to follow it to a special place. You accept the invitation and follow the path. The path leads you deep within the forest to the edge of a clearing . . . a magical open space surrounded by a ring of ancient redwoods, forming the outer circle, and by a sparkling stream, forming the inner circle. You cross the stream. You enter the clearing.

A woman approaches you: "The Mother of All Living is waiting. She has a gift for you. Come let us meet her in the center of the clearing." You see the Mother at a distance. You approach her with your arms at your sides. You feel no shame in her pres-

Self-nurturing for a woman requires an attitude of feminine valuing. It is enhanced by time in which you shift your attention to yourself . . . If you nurture yourself, the choices you make in your life will be conscious and empowered.
—Virginia Beane Rutter, *Celebrating Girls*

ence. Her eyes meet yours and in her gaze, you are recognized ... shaken ... and relieved. She embraces you and you become as you once were ... fully present and in love with yourself. She hands you a beautifully wrapped gift. As you open it, she speaks, "Daughter of Woman, dance the sadness of a lifetime for what could never be. And when your sadness is quieted, dance with her partner, gladness. For as deep a cavern as sorrow has carved within you that shall be your capacity for joy. Dance your gladness for what is now and will be forevermore.

"Daughter of Woman, receive again your birthright. Be interested in yourself. Delight in your own adventures. Explore everything in your world with wonder and awe. Gaze at the redness of an apple. Watch the water flow over the rocks in a stream. Listen to the rain dance. Count the peas on your plate. Ordinary life will be your teacher, your challenge, and your delight.

"Daughter of Woman, enjoy the privacy of quiet times, under-the-cover times, alone times to savor the events and experiences of your life. Touch the depths of your uniqueness. Use your time, energy, and attention in service of your own life. Remember yourself. Exist for yourself. Be desirable to yourself. The solitude of the universe pulsates through you. Be full of yourself."

A Vow of Faithfulness to Your Solitude

Imagine a woman who is available to herself. A woman who has crafted a fully formed solitude. Who chooses friends and lovers with the capacity to respect her solitude. Imagine yourself as this woman as you vow faithfulness to yourself.

Use the following activities to inspire, provoke, and give shape to your vow:

1. List the ways you nurture your own self-interest and self-involvement in your journal. If you are a parent, list the ways you nurture your daughter's self-interest and self-involvement.

2. Create two columns in your journal. In column 1, list the present-day challenges/opposition to nurturing your self-interest and self-involvement. In column 2, list the ways you will preserve allegiance to your solitude against each challenge/opposition.

3. In your journal note the memories, feelings, and sensations that come up as you read each of the following questions and as you imagine answering, "I Will" at your commitment ceremony.

> Will you sustain interest in yourself all the days of your life?
> Will you embrace your own life as teacher, healer, and challenge?
> Will you value your life's lessons above the prescriptions of experts?
> Will you befriend the solitude of your own life?

4. Allow women's vows to inspire your own. Highlight the phrases that resonate with your experience.

> I will allow myself unqualified, non-negotiable time.
>
> I vow to make space for the peaceful quiet of just being.
>
> I will seek to be still, so that I may hear God's voice and my own inner wisdom.
>
> I will find time to be alone and allow myself to do as I please in that time, with no recriminations.

I will be faithful to my need to sleep alone several nights a week and to wake up in my own bed on the days I choose for creative focus.

I will be faithful to my need for solitude between times of close ness with my beloved: to integrate the experiences of our rich intimacy, to return home to myself, and to breathe into my being the healing, challenge, and comfort of our closeness.

5. Take a deep breath. Gather phrases from the above exercises, sprinkle in some new ones, and compose a one- to three-sentence vow of faithfulness to your solitude.

Step 7 Reclaim Your Original Creativity

Remember Your Birthright

In the very beginning, the girl-child trusts her vision of the world and expresses it. With wonder and delight, she paints a picture, creates a dance, and makes up a song. To give expression to her creative impulses is as natural as her breathing. She creates in her own language-imagery-movement. She follows no script. She is not bound by the custom-ary way things have been expressed. Her creative intuition is original. She gathers all of life into her inner crucible and mixes it with her unique vision and experience. She loves the sounds, movements, ideas, images, and words that emerge from inside of her. Sometimes the creative impulse leads her to share her dance, her song, her picture. She is full of

Creativity is divine:
the virgin soul opens to the spirit
and conceives the divine child.
We cannot live without it.
It is the meaning of life,
this creative fire.
—MARION WOODMAN,
COMING HOME TO MYSELF

herself as she performs before audiences large and small. Other times she does not want to share her creative expression with anyone. She reads to herself, creates an art showing in the privacy of her bedroom, or dances with her beloved stuffed bears as her audience. The originality of the universe pulsates through her.

Pause to remember your original creativity and its expression: the time when you organized and directed the whole neighborhood's performance of a play you wrote; the time when you choreographed a "routine" and taught it to your girlfriends at a slumber party; or the time when you painted the sunset with berries while vacationing at the ocean with your grandparents.

If you do not remember your childhood, recall the creative expressions of your preadolescent daughter, granddaughter, or niece: the time when she made "sculptures" out of the cookie dough you taught her to prepare; the time when she made a collage out of the photos and memories of her best friend who had moved away; or the time when she asked to use your material scraps to design her first quilt. Allow your daughter, granddaughter, or niece to awaken memories of a time when you were full of your own creativity.

Choose whichever activity moves you: Write your parents a note of appreciation for nurturing your creative capacity. Write your daughters, granddaughters, or nieces a note celebrating their creative capacity. Write yourself a note appreciating the ways you nurture your own creative capacity.

Childhood's Hurtful Words and Experiences

Our capacity to create was judged as impractical, not good enough, and "outside the lines" by our parents and teachers. Very early on, our creative expressions were exposed to the competition-oriented comments of well-meaning others who judged our work as "better than" or "not as good as." Perfection became the goal, and anything less than perfect was thrown away. No longer was the emphasis on spontaneous expression rising from our own inner lives; product and performance took center stage. Creative expression became work assigned by parents and teachers with specific performance goals as its motivation. "Being creative" became a job to be done in its proper time and place. As our lives became cluttered with responsibility for others in the family and with the preoccupation with their needs, creativity became scheduled like everything else. Eventually, we lost touch with the spontaneous expressions of our inner lives. There was a particular way things were to be done, and if we dared to use our own colors, shapes, or movements, or to experiment with a brand-new way of doing something, we were scolded. We learned to stifle our creative impulses except in service of the careers and projects of our children and lovers, our friends and colleagues.

What words led to the repression of your creativity and the development of the self-just-like-everyone-else? Note the words in your journal. Choose whichever activity moves you: Write a note to your parents, expressing anger, frustration, or disappointment that they did not support your creative capacity to develop and flourish. Write a note to daughters, granddaughters, or nieces, acknowledging the ways you did not support their creative capacity to develop and flourish.

Healing Words and Experiences

Participate in the "Healthy Family Fantasy" in the quietness of your healing imagination. Enter into a childhood hoped for. . . . Place your childhood name in the blank.

Sometimes your sister reads to you from *The Book of Woman*. One school night after you finish your homework, she offers to read a story to you. You ask her to read "_____'s Favorite Room."

For as long as _____ can remember, in the apartments and houses she's lived in there has been a whole room filled with paint, crayons, glitter, and construction paper of all colors; glue, tape, stickers, and scissors of all kinds; sponges, brushes, and tongue depressors of all shapes; piles of old magazines, paper plates, and material scraps; containers of leaves and acorns, and other "Found Objects" from family walks and trips to the junkyard; a big table to work on; and large sheets of paper tacked up on all the walls, ready for the next adventure. Even when she lived in a very small apartment, her mom said, "What do we need a dining room for? We'll use in for our Play Womb and eat in the kitchen. To create is the food of the soul."

"Play Womb" is what _____'s mother calls the room because she believes that everyone can give birth to images, sounds, movements, and ideas—everyone, she said, even boys, have a "creative womb." Her father calls it the "Family Studio" because the room belongs to everyone in the family and "studio" sounded official to him—"We are all artists and everywhere we go, we will have a studio," he is always saying. And _____ calls it "Play Room" because she has so much fun whenever she is in there.

There is a big sign over the doorway that says, "Be Full of Yourself!" and a bowl of glitter attached to the wall like the holy water containers in a Catholic church. "This is our family church," her mom is always saying. "It is a holy place so we'll bless ourselves with glitter before entering." So reaches into the bowl and sprinkles herself with glitter every time she enters. There are only three rules in the playroom and they are easy to follow:

1. Cover the paints.

2. Be sure everything you use finds its way home to a pile, container, or shelf before you leave.

3. Move your painting to the "Drying Wall." Return for it within an hour. Hang it in the family gallery for public display or in your bedroom gallery for private display.

There is a sign-up sheet outside the "Play Room" so everyone in the family can spend private time in there each week. _____ always signs up for the after-school hours because she has lots to say after a long day, and she can't find the words to say it all—so she paints instead.

One day after school, _____ was very upset when she entered her special room. She painted rows and rows of girls and boys, and put a big *X* through each of them while saying, "Go away." She painted twenty-five *X*s and said twenty-five "Go away"s because there are twenty-five children plus her in the class. She was tired of them all, talking, yelling, fighting, and spilling—she wished she could be the only person in her class. After she painted the twenty-fifth *X* and said the twenty-fifth "Go away," _____ felt a lot better. She covered the paints, washed her hands, and then went into the kitchen to say "Hi" to her father. No one in the family bothers _____ until she finishes her afternoon time in the Play Room. They know she'll be in a much better mood after spending time in there!

Pause to remember a scene from childhood involving your creativity. If your creativity was supported in the scene, write it as you remember it. If your creativity was not supported in the scene you remember, rewrite it. Enter into the scene with your healing imagination: replace all critical words and persons with supportive ones. If the "Healthy Family Fantasy" touched or inspired you, read it again and again. Using it as your inspiration, write a "To Do" list for creating a "Play Womb"/"Family Studio"/"Play Room" in your home.

Descent and Rediscovery

Imagine yourself as a leaf let go of by an autumn tree . . . a leaf slowly and gradually descending toward the ground . . . its descent cushioned by the breath of life . . . a leaf touching the ground in the forest deep within your being. You rise from the ground, thanking the leaf for transporting you so gently.

Everything breathes in the forest. Savor the breath of life flowing in and around you. Inhale deeply as the breath rises from the rich earth beneath you. Release the breath into the cool and moist air around you. Your attention moves upward and you notice the trees reaching arm in arm for the sky. You become a tree. Your feet grow roots extending deep into the ground. Your arms become branches stretching high into the sky. You sway with the breeze. The birds of the forest dance with you as they leap from branch to branch. You see many things from your new height.

A nearby stream calls to you, "Come and play." In a moment, you are at the stream, splashing in its bouncing waters. As you are drying off in the warm sunlight pouring through the forest canopy, a path opens up before you and invites you to follow it to a special place. You accept the invitation and follow the path. The path leads you deep within the forest to the edge of a clearing . . . a magical open space surrounded by a ring of ancient redwoods, forming the outer circle, and by a sparkling stream, forming the inner circle. You cross the stream. You enter the clearing.

A woman approaches you: "The Mother of All Living is waiting. She has another gift for you. Come let us meet her in the center of the clearing." You see the Mother at a distance. You approach her with your arms at your sides. You feel no shame in her presence. Her eyes meet yours and in her gaze, you are recognized . . . shaken . . . and relieved. She embraces you and you become as you once were . . . fully present and in love with yourself. She hands you a beautifully wrapped gift. As you open it, she speaks: "Daughter of Woman, receive again your birthright. Trust your vision of the world and express it. With wonder and delight, paint a picture, create a dance, and make up a song. Create in your own language, imagery, and movement. Follow no script. You are not bound by the customary way things have been expressed. Your creative intuition is original. Gather all of life into your inner crucible, mix it with your unique vision and experience, and produce an original creation.

"Daughter of Woman, love the sounds, movements, ideas, images, and words emerging from inside of you. If the creative impulse leads you to share your dance, song, or picture; your design, quilt, or collage; your business, workshop, or sermon, be full of yourself as you 'perform' before audiences large and small. If you do not want to share your creative expression with anyone, read to yourself, create an art showing in the privacy of your bedroom, or dance with your beloved stuffed bears as your audience. The originality of the universe pulsates through you. Be full of yourself."

A Vow of Faithfulness to Your Creativity

Imagine a woman who follows her creative impulses. A woman who produces original creations. Who refuses to color inside someone else's lines. Imagine yourself as this woman as you vow faithfulness to yourself.

Use the following activities to inspire, provoke, and give shape to your vow:

1. List the ways you nurture your creativity in your journal. If you are a parent, list the ways you nurture your daughter's creativity.

2. Create two columns in your journal. In column 1, list the present-day challenges/opposition to nurturing your relationship to your creativity. In column 2, list the ways you will preserve allegiance to your creativity against each challenge/opposition.

3. In your journal note the memories, feelings, and sensations that are triggered as you read each of the following questions and as you imagine answering, "I Will" at a commitment ceremony.

> Will you love your creative impulses all the days of your life?
> Will you give expression to the words, shapes, images, and movements that emerge from within you?
> Will you celebrate your unique vision and experience?
> Will you produce original creations, refusing to color inside someone else's lines?

4. Allow women's vows to inspire your own. Highlight the phrases that resonate with your experience.

> I vow to let my beauty, creative expression, and bright light shine.
>
> I vow to sing my song as loud as I want to all the days of my life.
>
> I vow learn to play the piano, so that the light and the dark may dance together to my music.
>
> I vow to engage in creative expression three times a week and to establish "creative spaces" in my home to inspire and exhibit my expressions.

I promise to experiment with expressive media—verbal, visual, and movement—in order to find a medium for creative expression that works for me.

I vow to express myself creatively without wondering if it's the right way, the wrong way, or anyone else's way, and to allow myself the joy of sharing my accomplishments with trusted family and friends.

I will be faithful to my need for three days of complete surrender to my creative process: to follow its impulses, to nurture the business that sustains it, and to cultivate an audience to receive the fruit of my creative endeavors.

5. Take a deep breath. Gather phrases from the above exercises, sprinkle in some new ones, and compose a one- to three-sentence vow of faithfulness to your creativity.

Step 8 Reclaim Your Capacity to Be Full of Yourself!

Remember Your Birthright

In the very beginning, the girl-child wants to be seen and acknowledged. She feels good around people who look her in the eye, who ask her questions about her life, and who listen to her answers. She can tell when someone really sees and hears and likes her. To be around someone like that feels like eating her favorite flavor of ice cream. She smiles from her head to her toes. The girl-child can tell when someone doesn't see and hear and like her. To be around someone like that feels like eating lima beans. Lima beans are a pretty color and shape and lots of grown-ups like them, but she doesn't. Just like it's OK that she doesn't like certain foods, its OK that she doesn't like *everybody*. The girl-child only shows her projects to the special people in her life, the ones who make her smile. She tells them about her special dreams, except the very private ones, and lets them know about most of her special adventures. She loves it when they say, "WOW, you're fantastic!" or, "That's a colorful picture you drew. I like to look at it," or, "Your body is so very strong," or, "I'm so glad you are in my life!" Their words feel warm like the sun calling her out to play on a summer day. Their words say what she knows is true. She is a special girl: fantastic and strong, the maker of color-filled pictures, and fun to be around. The radiance of the universe pulsates through her.

Pause to remember your healthy desire for acknowledgment and recognition: the time when you hung all your second-grade paintings on the living room wall and sent invitations to the neighbors to come to your first art showing; the time when you asked all the Thanksgiving guests to listen to the stories you had written and to clap after each one; or the time you called your mother's best friend because you knew she'd listen to your ideas with the same interest she showed to adults.

If you do not remember your childhood, recall the healthy desire for acknowledgment and recognition expressed by your preadolescent daughter, granddaughter, or niece: the time she asked if the family could have a weekly "show and tell" time so everybody could be applauded; or the time when she wrote to the president about her ideas of how to help homeless people through the cold winter and called the White House because she didn't get a response soon enough to suit her. Allow your daughter, granddaughter, or niece to awaken memories of a time when you were full of yourself.

Choose whichever activity moves you: Write your parents a note of appreciation for nurturing your desire for acknowledgment and recognition. Write your daughters, granddaughters, or nieces a note celebrating their desire for acknowledgment and recognition. Write yourself a note of appreciation for the ways you nurture your own desire for acknowledgment and recognition.

Childhood's Hurtful Words and Experiences

Our desire for acknowledgment was judged as conceited, big-headed, self-inflated, and pompous by our families. Daily, we walked through a minefield of admonitions to be humble about our projects, dreams, accomplishments, and adventures, to be humble and quiet about ourselves at the expense of our own healthy self-celebration: Don't be so egotistical and full of yourself. Don't blow your own horn. Don't brag. Pretend you don't know what you know so you won't hurt his ego. Do well quietly so others won't feel intimidated by you. Don't be so obvious with your talents. Don't hurt other people's feelings by being so good at everything. You're too big for your britches. Stop showing off. Who do you think you are? Pride goeth before a fall. The constant repetition of these childhood commandments censored our natural desire for acknowledgment and recognition. We were required to be quiet about ourselves, to pretend that our ideas, projects, dreams, and talents were small and inconsequential so we wouldn't hurt other people's feelings and so we would be liked. We learned that girls are supposed to applaud for others, especially the boys.

What words required the relinquishment of your celebratory self and the development of the humble self? Note the words in your journal. Choose whichever activity moves you: Write a note to your parents expressing anger, frustration, or disappointment that they did not support your healthy desire for acknowledgment and recognition. Write a note to daughters, granddaughters, or nieces acknowledging how you did not support their healthy desire for acknowledgment and recognition.

Healing Words and Experiences

Participate in the "Healthy Family Fantasy" through play, movement, or in the quietness of your healing imagination. Trust your own impulse to sit quietly or to enact the fantasy. Enter into a childhood hoped for.... Place your childhood name in the blanks.

Our deepest fear is not that we are inadequate. Our deepest fear is that we are powerful beyond measure. It is our light, not our darkness that most frightens us. We ask ourselves, "Who am I to be brilliant, gorgeous, fabulous?" Actually who are you not to be? You are a child of God. Your playing small doesn't serve the world. We were born to make manifest the glory of God . . . with in us. It's not just in some of us; it's in everyone. And when we let our light shine, we unconsciously give other people the permission to do the same. As we are liberated from our fear, our presence automatically liberates others.
—MARIANNE WILLIAMSON

Sometimes your mother reads to you from *The Book of Woman*. One school night after you finish your homework, she offers to read a story to you. You ask her to read "_____'s Voice" so she does.

One Saturday night a month all of _____'s friends and the friends of her parents are invited over for "Show and Tell." _____'s mother is usually the Queen of Ceremonies because she always wanted to be a comedienne but her parents wanted her to learn to type until she got married. She didn't listen to her parents, never learned to type, and is the official comedienne of the family, the neighborhood, and the PTA. She starts off with the same words and actions every month:

"Be full of yourself.

Brag, boast, and show off.

Be pompous and big-headed.

Blow your own horn." (She blows a horn and passes it around!)

"Be loud about what you can do.

Be too big for your britches.

Have your cake and eat it too."

(She cuts the cake and passes it around!)

"Everyone gets a standing ovation because it takes courage to show and tell
in front of an audience. Sometimes it takes more courage for us grown-ups
to sing and dance, to share our ideas, and to read our words, but we do it
and we get a standing ovation too. Let's practice the ovation before we
begin." (Up and down until she thinks they've got it!)

One Saturday night, _____ was ready to sing her favorite country and western song. She had been practicing all week even though she
has known the words by heart since she was four years old. She was the
first one introduced by her mother and stepped onto the stage as her sister started the tape. At just the right moment she began to sing (with
Nancy Griffith's help) "Love at the Five-and-Dime." _____
invited every one to join in at the chorus:

"Dance a little closer to me.

Dance a little closer now.

Dance a little closer tonight cuz it's closing time and love's on sale
at Ivy's five-and-dime."

_____ got a standing ovation. At school they tell _____
that she "doesn't have a voice." She knows this isn't true. She does to
have a voice and she hears herself use it everyday. And _____

loves to sing. It makes her smile deep inside. So she doesn't listen to the people at school who tell her those things about her voice. She listens to her friends and family. She loves it when they say, "WOW, you're fantastic!" or, "That's a great song you taught us. I sang it all week," or, "Your face sparkles when you sing," or, "I'm so glad you are in my life!" Their words feel warm like the sun calling her out to play on a summer day. Their words say what she knows is true. She is a special girl with a special voice, and she'll keep singing because it makes her smile!

Pause to remember a scene from childhood involving your creativity. If your creativity was supported in the scene, write it as you remember it. If your creativity was not supported in the scene you remember, rewrite it. Enter into the scene with your healing imagination: replace all critical words and persons with supportive ones. If the "Healthy Family Fantasy" touched or inspired you, read it again and again. Using the "Healthy Family Fantasy" as your inspiration, write a "To Do" list for creating a "Show and Tell" evening for your friends and family.

Descent and Rediscovery

Imagine yourself as a leaf let go of by an autumn tree . . . a leaf slowly and gradually descending toward the ground . . . its descent cushioned by the breath of life . . . a leaf touching the ground in the forest deep within your being. You rise from the ground, thanking the leaf for transporting you so gently.

Everything breathes in the forest. Savor the breath of life flowing in and around you. Inhale deeply as the breath rises from the rich earth beneath you. Release the breath into the cool and moist air around you. Your attention moves upward and you notice the trees reaching arm in arm for the sky. You become a tree. Your feet grow roots extending deep into the ground. Your arms become branches stretching high into the sky. You sway with the breeze. The birds of the forest dance with you as they leap from branch to branch. You see many things from your new height.

A nearby stream calls to you, "Come and play." In a moment, you are at the stream, splashing in its bouncing waters. As you are drying off in the warm sunlight pouring through the forest canopy, a path opens up before you and invites you to follow it to a special place. You accept the invitation and follow the path. The path leads you deep within the forest to the edge of a clearing . . . a magical open space surrounded by a ring of ancient redwoods, forming the outer circle, and by a sparkling stream, forming the inner circle. You cross the stream. You enter the clearing.

195

A woman approaches you: "The Mother of All Living is waiting. She has a final gift for you. Come let us meet her in the center of the clearing." You see the Mother at a distance. You approach her with your arms at your sides. You feel no shame in her presence. Her eyes meet yours and in her gaze, you are recognized . . . shaken . . . and relieved. She embraces you and you become as you once were . . . fully present and in love with yourself. She hands you a beautifully wrapped gift. As you open it, she speaks: "Daughter of Woman, receive again your birthright. Imagine into being a life that fosters the deepening of your capacity to love your body, its needs and sensations; to express your truth and perceptions, your feelings and creative potential; to cultivate your solitude; and to celebrate yourself. Imagine into being a community of advocates, a chosen family available to nurture your connection to yourself and to applaud your fullness. Daughter of Woman, refuse to turn toward your own children with the words once spoken to you. Imagine into being an environment in which their natural capacities are supported to develop and flourish.

"Daughter of woman, the clearing is not your home. Return to your own folk and spread the good news: it is right and good that you are woman. The radiance of the universe pulsates through you. Be full of yourself!"

A Vow of Faithfulness to Your Fullness

Imagine a woman who refuses to diminish her life so others will feel better. A woman who brings the fullness of her experience and wisdom into each relationship. Who expects others to be blessed and challenged by her presence in their lives. Imagine yourself as this woman as you vow faithfulness to yourself.

Use the following activities to inspire, provoke, and give shape to your vow:

1. List the ways you nurture your desire for recognition and acknowledgment in your journal. If you are a parent, list the ways you nurture your daughter's desire for recognition and acknowledgment.

2. Create two columns in your journal. In column 1, list the present-day challenges and opposition to nurturing your desire for recognition and acknowledgment. In column 2, list the ways you will preserve allegiance to your desire for recognition and acknowledgment in the face of opposition.

3. In your journal note the memories, feelings, and sensations that are triggered as you read each of the following questions and as you imagine answering, "I Will" in a commitment ceremony.

Will you choose to be full of yourself all the days of your
    life?
Will you honor your desire for acknowledgment and
    recognition?
Will you surround yourself with friends who applaud your
    fullness?

4. Allow women's vows to inspire your own. Highlight the phrases
   that resonate with your experience.

   I will love myself powerfully!

   I vow to be true to myself and share my gifts through the avenue
   of joy.

   I vow to establish "creative spaces" in my home to inspire and
   exhibit my expressions.

   I will allow myself the joy of sharing my accomplishments with
   trusted family and friends.

   I vow to act with the full power I possess as an independent,
   intelligent, and intuitive woman.

   I vow to accept, trust, honor, and express
   all that arises and flows from every part of
   my being.

   I vow to live up to the name I gave myself:
   Valerie Larenne, Queen of My Universe and
   Ruler of My Own Destiny!

   I vow to tell myself daily "I love you" and
   know in the depths of my soul that I have
   been wanted from the beginning of time.

*There have always been women who
    remember the old ways.
Women who refuse to please others
by becoming smaller than they are.
Women who take space
with their thoughts and feelings,
their needs and desires,
their anger and their dreams.
Women full of themselves.*

—PLR

I vow to let go of the notion that I am inferior and that I cannot do anything of value, no matter how hard I try and no matter what I achieve.

5. Take a deep breath. Gather phrases from the above exercises, sprinkle in some new ones, and compose a one- to three-sentence vow of faithfulness to your desire for acknowledgment and recognition.

Step 9 Compose the Final Draft of Your Vow

Read back through your writings from the previous eight exercises. Rewrite your eight vow fragments in one place. Add new ideas as they come to you. Read through each list of fragments and additions, editing, refining, and discarding as you are moved. There is no "right" way to compose a vow. Read the following vows. Many women start with the eight capacities and then move to other areas of importance to them. What else wants to be acknowledged in your vow? Add it now. You may decide to set aside everything you've written up to this point. Trust your creative urges.

Before the Mother of All Living and my sacred sisters, I, Annette LaPorte, vow to embrace my life and be faithful to that which matters to me; to simply accept, trust, honor, love, and express all that arises and flows from every part of my being. So be it.

I, Maria Elena, vow to let go of the notion that I am inferior and that I cannot do anything of value, no matter how hard I try and no matter what I achieve. I vow to love, accept, and esteem my whole being and then let my beauty, creative expression, and bright light shine. I vow to be true to myself and share my gifts through the avenue of joy.

I, Donna Strachan-Ledbetter, vow the following in order to celebrate the fullness of who I am: to tell myself each day "I love you" and know in the depths of my soul that I have been wanted from the beginning of time; to practice letting go of the incessant critical voices of myself and of others; to make space for the peaceful quiet of just being; and finally, before this year draws to a close, to begin again to learn and play the piano, so that the light and the dark may dance together to my music.

I, Mary Bolling, vow to speak in a voice clear and strong; to look upon myself with a merciful eye; to notice and accept the feelings my body gives me as trustworthy information, to breathe into them, and then to choose how I will respond; to state clearly when something doesn't work for me and to create an acceptable alternative; to look with loving kindness upon my shame about my body curiosity and exploration while growing up; to set aside thirty minutes three times a week for soul-play.

I, Lacy Laura, vow faithfully to: Believe I was born a divine child of Life with innate goodness. Honor my physical, spiritual, and emotional needs as I see fit. Believe I am loving and lovable. Honor my past experiences and choices. Believe I have a right to all my feelings. Honor my life-spark: that resilient, brilliant person inside. Believe I am a worthwhile person, that I have a right to exist and flourish in all my capacities. I vow to sit in sacred circles of women to remind me when I forget my goodness.

I, Valerie Larenne, vow: to honor and acknowledge my body as a vital and sacred resource through regular exercise, rest, and nourishing food; to reclaim the joy in using my body to explore the world and experience the limitlessness of my horizon; to assert my needs and act with the full power I possess as an independent, intelligent, and intuitive woman; to own, explore, and celebrate my sexuality as a vital, natural, and healthy resource; to honor the inherent validity of all my feelings; to act courageously in speaking my truths as loudly or as softly as they need to be spoken; to continue exploring my creativity through painting, photography, and tending the roses in my garden; to live up to the name I gave myself—Valerie Larenne—Queen of My Universe and Ruler of My Own Destiny!

Write your final vow on a separate piece of paper. Review it monthly and renew it yearly. When faced with life challenges, review your personal vow. Regularly cultivate your partnership with yourself. It is the best investment you can make in whole, healthy, and joyful life.

Step 10 Design a Ceremony of Commitment

Many women choose to adapt the "vow of faithfulness" Ceremony of Commitment in chapter 2 to culminate the "Descending into the Richness" process. Others create a personal ceremony based on their life principles or spiritual beliefs. If this is your choice, allow Amy's ceremony to inspire you. To prepare for whatever ceremony you use, recopy your vow on a special piece of paper and choose a symbolic item such as a ring, earring, stone, feather, or scarf; or recopy it on the "Vow" page at the back of this book as a tangible reminder of your vow. Bring your vow and symbolic item to the ceremony.

Amy's Ceremony

From early childhood, Amy's one all-consuming fantasy had been of standing under the *chupah* (wedding canopy) with her beloved. Tired of this fantasy and the romance and relationship addiction it inspired, she included the chupah in a private ceremony witnessed by women friends. Here is the outline of Amy's ceremony:

1. Light the Shabbat candles and chant the blessing in Hebrew, including G-d's name as female and as "Queen of the Universe." At the end of the prayer, change the word *shabbat* to *ha yom*, making the blessing for "Today."

2. Four women hold the corners of the chupah, the wedding canopy, over my head.

3. I recite my vow:

    > "I, Amy Stern Fishbach, vow that:
    > As I so love the moon,
    > Shall I so love myself.

And as I so love the sound of running creek water,
Shall I so love myself and the sound of my Inner Voice.
And as I so love special stones
And a certain way sun falls through the leaves,
Shall I so love what makes me special to myself.

I will remember that by myself
I have everything I need and
I am enough."

4. Walk around photographs of myself three times.

5. Recite the Hebrew prayer I invented for myself, addressed to G-d: *"Anachu ovdeem b'yah-chad."* ("We work together.") Ask the women, *"Nachon?"* ("Right?") All the women reply, *"Nachon!"* ("Right!")

6. With my foot, smash the tree bark, representing the broken years of my life. *"L'chaim!"* ("To life!")

Daughter of Woman, remain loyal to yourself. Regardless

Patricia Lynn Reilly holds a Master of Divinity degree from Princeton Theological Seminary and a postgraduate certification in Women's Spirituality and Feminist Theology from the Women's Theological Center. As the founder of Open Window Creations, she conducts women's spirituality, creativity, and self-esteem workshops and publishes inspirational books and resources. Patricia is the author of:

Imagine a Woman in Love with Herself: Embracing Your Wisdom and Wholeness (Conari Press, 1999)

Be Full of Yourself: The Journey from Self-Criticism to Self-Celebration (Open Window Creations, 1998)

A God Who Looks Like Me: Discovering a Woman-Affirming Spirituality (Ballantine, 1995)

Companion Resources

Patricia Lynn Reilly offers a variety of workshops, retreats, and presentations based on the content of her books. She has also developed woman-affirming resources to enhance the reader's experience of her work, including:

"I Promise Myself" Vow-Composition Workbooks

- ∽ The Essential Vow of Faithfulness

- ∽ Companion Vows for All Seasons of Life

- ∽ Remembering Yourself: Composing a Vow for Marriage and/or the Birth of a Child

- ∽ Gathering the Gifts: Composing a Vow to Support Conscious Transitions

- ∽ Discovering the Way Home: Composing a Vow to Reclaim Your Natural Resources

- ∽ Descending into the Richness: Composing a Vow to Reclaim Your Natural Capacities

"Home Is Always Waiting Meditation" audiocassette

If you would like a schedule of upcoming events and a brochure of companion resources, write or e-mail:

Open Window Creations
P. O. Box 8615
Berkeley, California 94707
E-mail: patricia@openwindowcreations.com
Web site: **www.openwindowcreations.com**

To Our Readers

CONARI PRESS publishes books on topics ranging from spirituality, personal growth, and relationships to women's issues, parenting, and social issues. Our mission is to publish quality books that will make a difference in people's lives—how we feel about ourselves and how we relate to one another. We value integrity, compassion, and receptivity, both in the books we publish and in the way we do business.

As a member of the community, we sponsor the Random Acts of Kindness™ Foundation, the guiding force behind Random Acts of Kindness™ Week. We donate our damaged books to nonprofit organizations, dedicate a portion of our proceeds from certain books to charitable causes, and continually look for new ways to use natural resources as wisely as possible.

Our readers are our most important resource, and we value your input, suggestions, and ideas about what you would like to see published. Please feel free to contact us to request our latest book catalog or to be added to our mailing list.

CONARI PRESS
2550 Ninth Street, Suite 101
Berkeley, California 94710-2551
800-685-9595   510-649-7175
fax: 510-649-7190   e-mail: conari@conari.com
www.conari.com

My Vow of Faithfulness